THE EMPERORS OF CHINA

TREASURES OF THE WORLD

THE EMPERORS OF CHINA

by
Christopher Hibbert

Select
BOOKS

SELECT BOOKS
A Division of Time-Life Books, B.V. Amsterdam

First published in Great Britain, 1982

Treasures of the World was created and produced by Tree Communications, Inc., New York, N.Y.

THE AUTHOR: Christopher Hibbert, a Fellow of the Royal Society of Literature, is the author of many biographies and historical works, including *The Great Mutiny*, *The Dragon Wakes: China and the West*, and *Days of the French Revolution*.

CONSULTANTS FOR THIS BOOK: *Robert D. Mowry* is curator of the Mr. and Mrs. John D. Rockefeller 3rd Collection of Asian Art at The Asia Society in New York. *Wan-go Weng*, a writer, film-maker, and photographer, was born in China and is a collector of Chinese paintings and calligraphy. *Paul Clifford*, one of the first Western students at Peking University, is a lecturer in Chinese history at the University of London.

SERIES CONSULTANTS: Dr. Ulrich Hiesinger has taught art history at Harvard College and at the Uniuversity of Pennsylvania and has been guest curator at the Philadelphia Museum of Art.

Joseph J. Thorndike, Jr., a senior editor of American Heritage Publishing Company, was the founder and editor of *Horizon* magazine and is a former managing editor of *Life*.

ISBN: 7054 1000 5

ABOVE: *This winged lion of bronze, gold and silver was cast in the eleventh or twelfth century* A.D.

COVER: *The silk tapestry "dragon robe" of Ch'ing dynasty emperor Shun-chich signified his power.*

TITLE PAGE: *Ming dynasty emperor Wan-li, on a richly outfitted horse, towers over his ministers.*

OVERLEAF: *An elephant-drawn cart, possibly carrying a concubine, is part of an imperial procession.*

CONTENTS

CHOU DYNASTY 350 B.C.

HAN DYNASTY c. A.D. 100

T'ANG DYNASTY A.D. 700

China's present-day borders are indicated on the large map at right. The smaller maps show the borders of six dynasties, each at its greatest extent, and the capitals of those dynasties.

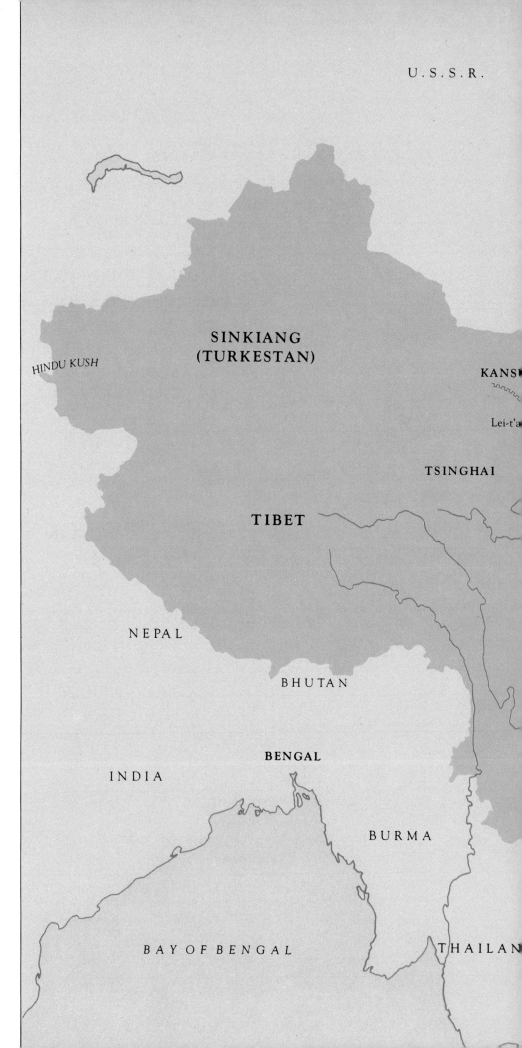

U.S.S.R.

SINKIANG
(TURKESTAN)

HINDU KUSH

KANS

Lei-t'a

TSINGHAI

TIBET

NEPAL

BHUTAN

BENGAL

INDIA

BURMA

BAY OF BENGAL

THAILAN

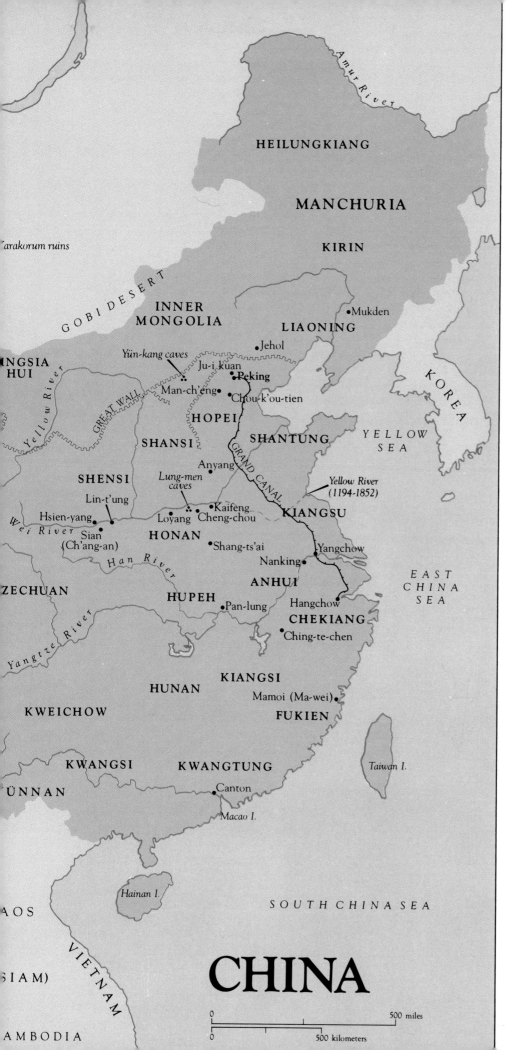

HEILUNGKIANG

MANCHURIA

KIRIN

Amur River

Karakorum ruins

GOBI DESERT

INNER
MONGOLIA

•Mukden

LIAONING

•Jehol

Yün-kang caves

NINGSIA
HUI

GREAT WALL

Yellow River

Ju-i kuan
•Peking
Man-ch'eng
•Chou-k'ou-tien

HOPEI

KOREA

SHANSI

SHANTUNG

YELLOW
SEA

SHENSI

Anyang

Lung-men
caves

GRAND CANAL

Lin-t'ung
Hsien-yang
Sian
(Ch'ang-an)

Loyang
Kaifeng
Cheng-chou

Yellow River
(1194-1852)

KIANGSU

Wei River

HONAN

•Shang-ts'ai

Yangchow

SZECHUAN

Han River

Nanking•

EAST
CHINA
SEA

HUPEH

•Pan-lung

ANHUI

Hangchow

CHEKIANG

Yangtze River

•Ching-te-chen

KIANGSI

HUNAN

Mamoi (Ma-wei)•

KWEICHOW

FUKIEN

YÜNNAN

KWANGSI

KWANGTUNG

Taiwan I.

•Canton

Macao I.

Hainan I.

SOUTH CHINA SEA

LAOS

VIETNAM

(SIAM)

CHINA

0   500 miles
0   500 kilometers

CAMBODIA

Kaifeng•

SUNG DYNASTY c. A.D. 1000

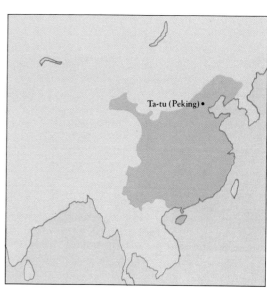

Ta-tu (Peking)•

MING DYNASTY c. A.D. 1580

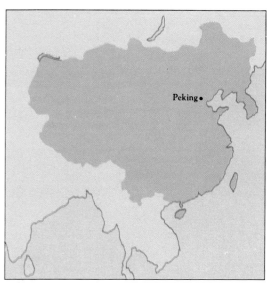

Peking•

CH'ING DYNASTY A.D. 1760-1842 and 1858

9

I

BRONZE AGE LEGENDS

OF THE SHANG AND CHOU

China's ancient history merges into myth. In the beginning the world was an egg. When the egg cracked open, the top of the shell grew to become the sky, the lower part became the earth, and out of the middle stepped a man P'an-ku, who lived for eighteen thousand years. Helped by a dragon, a phoenix, a unicorn, and a tortoise, P'an-ku worked hard, cutting the earth into shape, making the valleys and the mountains. And when he died his flesh became the earth's soil, his blood became the seas and rivers, his eyes the sun and moon, his breath the wind, his voice thunder. The parasites that fed upon his body became the ancestors of the human race. Such is the story told to Chinese children, over the generations.

In the earliest times the people that developed from P'an-ku's parasites were ruled by such supernaturally endowed hero-kings as Fu-hsi, who taught men how to hunt and fish, to rear animals for food, and to write, who instructed them in philosophy and music and in living harmoniously with women in marriage.

In Chinese mythology, supermen and legendary emperors such as Yü the Great, enthroned opposite, created the universe and brought civilization to mankind.

Other great rulers founded dynasties that lasted thousands of years and guided their people into an ever more civilized life.

These rulers gave the people institutions, which men in later times looked back upon as models of perfection. They encouraged piety and sacrifices to the gods, regard for the family and veneration for ancestors; these have remained among the basic continuities of Chinese culture. There were other constant features, too, among them an underlying misogyny. Except for an occasional empress or powerful concubine, women at all levels of Chinese society and all periods of imperial history have been held in low regard.

No one knows when Chinese civilization began. The hallmarks of civilization—systematic agriculture, a settled way of life, villages—existed in China by at least 3000 B.C., perhaps later than in Mesopotamia. But these centuries remain mysterious. The mists of legend begin to clear with the appearance of Yü the Great, who created a vast system of drainage canals to protect the country from the floods that had previously inundated it and who, in the twenty-first century B.C., founded the Hsia dynasty. But of that dynasty virtually nothing else is known apart from a list of its emperors, and skeptical historians have doubted its very existence. Some once doubted, too, the stories told of the Shang dynasty, which had, so it was said, succeeded the Hsia in the sixteenth century B.C. Yet, in the case of the Shang, modern archaeology has proved the skeptics wrong.

One of the very earliest forms of man had lived in China. In the 1920s at Chou-k'ou-tien, near Peking, fossilized bone remains were found—mostly skulls of men and women who had walked upright, used stone tools and fire for cooking between 250,000 and 500,000 years ago. Peking Man, as he is called, was indigenous. The Chinese were not, as scholars had supposed, descended from people who had migrated from the Middle East. Later excavations unearthed even earlier human fossils; the earliest, found in 1976, was no less than 1,700,000 years old.

Meanwhile other scholars were unearthing the ancient Shang

A performer with a wooden beam strikes the chung-bells made in sets. Music was important in the courts of Chinese kings, who believed that the clear, vigorous tones of bronze bells would entertain and pacify their subjects. This rubbing is from a tomb in Shantung, in northeastern China.

civilization of China, the first one definitely known to have existed. In the late nineteenth century, scholars noticed that certain old bones, which were traditionally ground to powder for a cure-all known as Dragon Bone, had strange symbols and characters carved upon them. These were ancient oracle bones used to foretell future events: when incised and heated, the bones cracked in a significant way. Their date was about 1300 B.C., during the time of the Shang, and they came from the area around Anyang, about eighty miles north of the Yellow River in Honan province.

Partly because of traditionalists who condemned archaeologists as heathen grave robbers, excavation of the tombs at Anyang did not begin until 1928. But then, however, thousands more oracle bones were revealed and with them a vocabulary of no less than 2,500 characters, the earliest known form of the written language of China, and probably the oldest surviving language in the world. It was undoubtedly in use many centuries before any of the bones were carved. Modified and simplified, it is still in use today.

At the same time the excavations at Anyang revealed a cultivated society whose artists and craftsmen had reached a level of virtuosity unmatched in the West for two thousand years. These artisans established China's enduring esteem for beautiful objects, for those treasures that became so uniquely Chinese in their style and so highly prized not only for the intrinsic value of their materials—jade, bronze, gold, porcelain, and silk—but for the exquisite craftsmanship unrivaled in history.

The Shang masters were expert carvers in marble as well as limestone and wood; they were gifted makers and painters of pottery, and, above all, masterly workers in the two classic Chinese materials—jade and bronze, prized even above gold. Their bronzes were among the finest masterpieces of early Chinese civilization, comparable to the greatest works of the European Renaissance. (In Greece and the Near East, bronze casting began in about 2500 B.C.—but nowhere rivaled Shang proficiency.) To

A messenger, below right, hands a gift to an official of a legendary emperor, seated, at top, on his throne in a bamboo-shaded pavilion. This scene, like the one opposite, is from a scroll probably painted in the eighteenth century A.D.

decorate their bronzes, Shang metallurgists and artists developed a superbly intricate design unique to China–the fearsome *t'ao-t'ieh*, or animal mark motif, a head viewed from the front.

The Shang ruling class had sole control of the costly and complex technology of casting, and their craftsmen used their arcane knowledge to create not only sophisticated bronze ritual vessels but also bronze weapons to buttress their authoritarian rule. In Shang society, which was probably based on slavery, life was cheap. The tombs of Shang rulers contain mass sacrifices–human beings, presumably slaves or prisoners of war, in rows alongside chariots and bronze objects for use in the afterlife.

The aristocrats of this ancient civilization, riding in their chariots, no doubt dressed in rich silks and furs, owed allegiance to a king who, from his capital, ruled the country through a hierarchy of officials and supervised its trade. At least six capital cities in addition to Anyang have been identified and one of these, Cheng-chou, has also been excavated. From these cities the Shang exercised their authority over a wide area around Honan until they were conquered in the eleventh century B.C. by a former client state on the northwestern frontier whose ruler, King Wu, established a new dynasty, the Chou.

From the literature left by the Chou it is possible to form a picture of a society at once highly organized, highly religious, and highly cultured. Most people still lived on the land, often in pits underground. But in the cities, at court, and in the houses of the rich, the handicrafts and metal implements were as sophisticated as they were beautiful. Copper coins, with square holes for stringing, came into use in the time of the Chou.

The Chou kings seem to have ruled efficiently and justly; yet they were always conscious that although they had received the "Mandate of Heaven" to rule "All Beneath The Sky," that mandate could be taken away from them. It had already been taken away from the Shang, whose last king was a wicked and merciless man with a favorite concubine as cruel as himself.

Thus was born that traditional view of Chinese history as a

series of dynastic cycles: a strong, just ruler assumes power; his dynasty flourishes; then, after a period of reckless ambition followed by decline and corruption, it is overthrown by another whose history follows the same pattern. This is a limited and strictly political view of history. Chinese history is also the story of Chinese culture spreading southward and the development of central China as the nation's granary, of private industry flourishing in the tenth through thirteenth centuries under a dynasty called the Sung only to fade away in later centuries, of revolutionary advances in agriculture and dramatic growths in population. Yet, although Chinese society was never changeless, the cyclical pattern of the dynasties is clearly discernible.

Equally discernible are the gradations of change—but change within a framework of certain immutable attitudes and ideas that are essentially Chinese and against a background of art and culture that is extraordinarily constant. This continuity, indeed, is the most striking aspect of Chinese civilization. It is not old when compared with the civilizations of India and the Middle East: King Cheops' pyramid at Giza was built more than eight hundred years before the Hsia dynasty is said to have been founded; Troy flourished; and the palace of Knossos rose on Crete long before the Shang civilization appeared. But the earlier civilizations did not endure; the Chinese did.

Following the Shang, the Chou kings reigned for more than eight hundred years. In the earlier centuries their power increased and their influence spread to the north and northeast far beyond Honan, Hopei, and Shantung, as well as large parts of Shansi, Shensi, and Anhui. Knowing nothing of the cultures to the west, they believed themselves unique. China they knew as *Chung-kuo*, the Middle Kingdom, beyond which on all sides lived barbarians. But in the eighth century B.C., weakened by military campaigns against refractory domains within and the barbarians who continually assaulted the scattered fortifications along the frontiers, the Chou empire disintegrated into numerous small, belligerent states. During this period of decline and

King Wu, the first ruler of the Chou dynasty, which commenced in the eleventh century B.C., *hears a sage read the astrological chart spread out between them. The guard at left holds an imperial halberd, the guard at right a spear.*

FOR THE LOVE OF SILK

Of all the treasures China harbored in its centuries of isolation from the West none was more mysterious to outsiders, more intoxicating in its beauty and value than silk. At some unknown time, perhaps as early as five thousand years before Christ, the Chinese learned to cultivate the mulberry silkworm and to unwind the cocoon the worms spin every spring and to retrieve its lovely, gossamer thread. Dyed and woven into fabric, silk served as one of the mainstays of the Chinese economy: the Chinese used bolts of silk as currency, which they hoarded in troubled times along with gems and gold. Starting in the second century B.C., the Chinese exported silk fabric to an eager market in Asia and Europe. Caravans of camels and yaks trekked four thousand miles through deserts and mountain ranges to Asian cities and the Mediterranean, where the cargo was shipped to points west. In Rome, delighted patricians decked themselves in the exotic fabric, undeterred by outrageous prices—by the third century A.D. silk was worth almost its weight in gold. To ensure their monopoly on this fabulously profitable trade, the Chinese forbade the export of silkworm eggs on pain of death. The Japanese managed to obtain some worms in the third century, and a Chinese princess (right) illegally carried out a few worms when she went as a bride to central Asia in the fifth century. A pair of monks once and for all broke the Chinese monopoly about 550, smuggling eggs inside a cane to the Byzantine court at Constantinople and founding the industry there. Though the Byzantines became adept at making silk, wealthy buyers still preferred the superior Chinese product. The silk caravans continued to wend their way across Asia until the Muslim conquest of Persia sealed the route in the eighth century.

Sent to marry the king of Khotan in central Asia, this Chinese princess, so the story goes, defied an imperial edict and took silkworms with her, hidden in her crown. This portrait of her, on wood, was made in Khotan in the seventh century.

unrest China's great philosophies emerged and flourished. Of these, Taoism, which later became a religion as well as a philosophy; Legalism, an authoritarian, work-centered kind of political philosophy that was to be closely associated with the state of Ch'in; and Confucianism were by far the most influential.

The founder of Taoism, according to tradition, is Lao-tzu, born early in the sixth century B.C. For a time he was a librarian in the Chou archives, but when the power of his masters declined he retired from his position and from the world. He decided to walk westward and on his way a customs official in a mountain pass persuaded him to set down his ideas. He did so in a short book of some five thousand characters, known as the *Tao-te Ching*, or *Book of the Way and Virtue*.

Lao-tzu may never have existed, and the *Tao-te Ching* is more likely to be an anthology of Taoist precepts compiled in the fourth century B.C. than to have been inscribed by his brush. But it is still widely read in China as the classical work in the thought of Taoism. *Tao* means The Way, and the way to survival, Taoism teaches, is the path of submission to the principles of nature. "The hard and the strong are the comrades of death," says the *Tao-te Ching*. "The supple and weak are the comrades of life." By "sitting and forgetting" and "fasts of the mind," by breathing exercises and self-induced trances, the Taoist could become one with the universe. Yet Taoism was as much a philosophy of protest as of submission: power, riches, and fame were in themselves worthless; those who possessed them were not to be honored.

In sharp contrast to Taoism, Confucianism not only was concerned with political problems but also taught that men should play the parts assigned to them in an authoritarian society. Confucius himself, or K'ung-fu-tzu to use his Chinese name, was born about 551 B.C. in what is now Shantung province. He was a well-educated man, perhaps an aristocrat, but he never achieved the high political office he thought he deserved. Still, he loved music and singing and enjoyed the pleasures of country life–riding, swimming, and archery—and he recognized that food and sex were the two natural desires of man.

Inspired by his character and his ideas, his disciples compiled the *Lun-yü*, or *Analects*, after his death. From these, the master's answers to his students' questions, we learn of the philosophy that was to dominate Chinese society for centuries to come. This philosophy implied that while men were naturally good, their virtue had to be brought out by a ruler whose authority must be obeyed but whose government must be just.

One of the foremost champions of these beliefs was the philosopher Meng-tzu, the only Chinese philosopher, apart from his master, to be known in the West by a Latinized form of his name, Mencius. Although Mencius was an ardent disciple of Confucius, his reinterpretation of the master was wide-ranging: the concepts of Confucianism owe as much to Mencius as to the sage himself. Like Confucius before him, Mencius, born around 372 B.C., traveled about in search of the high office that was never bestowed upon him. Unlike Confucius, though, he insisted that a government must govern with the consent of the people.

When Mencius died in 289 B.C., the royal house of Chou had long since lost its empire, and the period known as the Warring States was drawing to its close. The cycle of imperial history was about to turn once more. But during the Shang and Chou, the distinctly Chinese culture that was to dominate the subsequent two thousand years of imperial history had already taken shape. Though the Shang kings ruled over only a tiny part of north China, their bronzes and jades reached the heights of artistic and technological achievement. Exquisitely made, they nevertheless reflect the exuberant energy of the society that prized them. Their design is at once primitive and elegant, their uses both practical and mystical. No one looking closely at them could doubt that they are inimitably Chinese. They are the very fountainhead of an artistic tradition that was to continue for many centuries. They are treasures now to the world at large—the more so as ancient emblems of a civilization that still endures.

Craftsmen of 1000 B.C. *fashioned this ceremonial ax from an inlaid bronze handle and a jade blade, thus combining the materials most beloved by the ancient Chinese.*

Jades representing heaven (left) and earth (above) were important in lavish burials of ancient China. Though their exact meanings remain a mystery, the disk, called a pi, *and the square column, a* ts'ung, *were often placed inside coffins.*

The royal and aristocratic members of ancient China's Shang and Chou dynasties demanded two materials that epitomized wealth and power: jade and bronze. By 1500 B.C. artists had learned to cast bronze, to work jade, and to fashion both into objects of great beauty. Vested with mystical meaning, jade and bronze were also heavy with religious and even political significance. Jade was especially important in laying powerful ancestors to rest and paying respects to them.

The Chinese believed that man possessed twin souls that parted company at death—one to dwell in a tomb, the other to ascend. While the earthbound soul had to be placated and provided for, the heavenly spirit, able to affect the fortunes of the living, demanded veneration. Both required sacrifice (often human) and splendid offerings of jade and bronze.

Chinese emperors valued jade more highly than Western kings did gold and silver. Since the precious stone does not occur in China, thousands of laborers had to quarry blocks of it from faraway lands while others, usually women, searched for pebbles of jade in rivers. Jadesmiths could not carve the hard stone, but worked it painstakingly with abrasives such as quartz sand. Besides being beautiful (its coloring varies from white to green to gray), jade was smooth, heavy, and resonant: wealthy Chinese had small bits of it sewn into their robes, which then made lovely tinkling sounds as they moved about.

The Chinese believed that jade prolonged life (they actually powdered the stone and ate it) and reserved the finest specimens—representing the heavens, earth, and protection in the afterlife—for elaborate burials. Although jades gradually became more decorative and less ritualistic, the mystique held beyond the last centuries of the Chou dynasty. When Chuang-tzu, a philosopher of the late fourth century B.C., told his disciples that "Heaven and earth will be my inner and outer coffins, the sun and moon my twin *pi* disks, the stars and planets my beads," he was describing the symbolic jades vital to a proper burial.

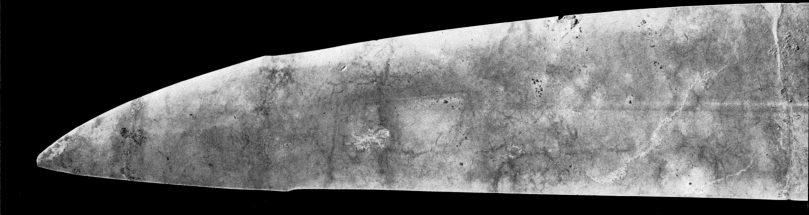

Blood never stained the sharp translucent edge of this three-foot jade blade, or ge. Unlike lethal knives of bronze or iron, the ge was the symbolic weapon of guardians who were buried alive in pits beneath the coffins of royalty. Made from one piece of jade in about 1500 B.C., this ge was broken into several pieces before it was placed in a grave at Pan-lung on the Yangtze River. According to the beliefs of the time, such ceremonial jades had to be "killed" in this way before interment.

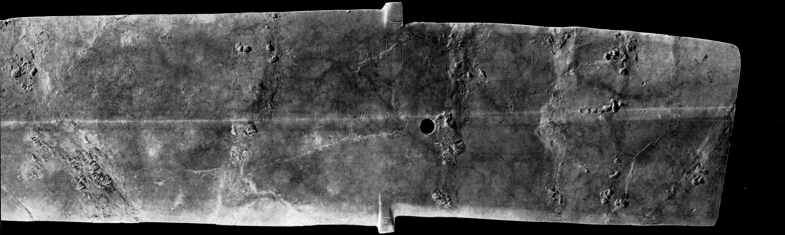

TIGER DECORATED WITH A GRANULAR PATTERN

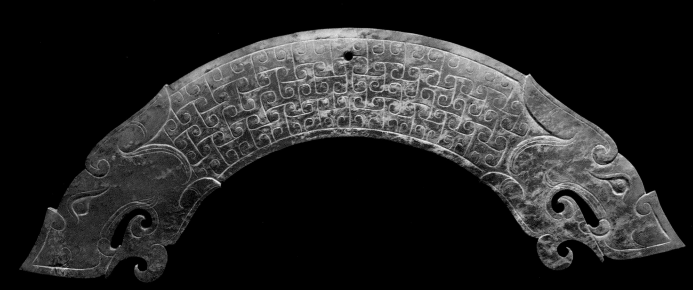

POINTED DRAGONS' HEADS AT EACH END OF A SCROLL-COVERED PENDANT

TRANSLUCENT HAWK WITH WINGS OUTSPREAD

As the centuries passed, the Chinese learned to work jade into complex and sometimes playful ornaments. By the late Chou dynasty (c.770 B.C.), the jade pendants such as these were wrought in the shapes of stylized animals. In this era exquisite jades—once used primarily in royal burials—adorned the robes of the rich and powerful.

HINGED CAT AND BIRD

Two tigers form the ends of an elaborate jade pendant of the fourth century B.C. *The curved tails, urn-shaped centerpiece, and elaborate*

scrollwork are characteristic of later Chou dynasty jades, which were more fanciful than the earlier ones used in somber burial sites.

Although fine bronzes appeared in China about two thousand years after the first foundries were operating in Europe, they are unsurpassed, even by their Western predecessors. A precious alloy chiefly of copper and tin, the bronze was forged with a reverence befitting the contexts in which it was often used. Having already mastered the fiery creation of fine ceramics, the Chinese brought special knowledge to the complex "piece-mold" production of bronze. The process involved many steps, principally the sculpting of detailed clay molds, which were lashed together with leather straps or straw rope and filled with molten metal. Abstract designs and two-headed animal masks were worked into the clay and directly cast into the finished piece. Once the bronze had cooled, the clay molds were removed and the surface had only to be polished. Bronze made superb weapons and agricultural implements, but even the crudest axes and blades had symbolic meanings beyond their practical purposes. Inscribed with records of significant events, and dedicated to rulers and deified ancestors, bronzes were historical documents that legitimized authority. Possessing the right bronze could make a man a king—in much the same way as the legendary King Arthur was crowned upon drawing the sword Excalibur from an anvil. All of the bronzes on these pages were recovered from the tombs of ancient China's most powerful men and women.

Its face bearing a sardonic grin, this ax was found in a tomb along with forty-eight decapitated skeletons: human sacrifices buried in Shantung province in northeastern China about 1180 B.C.

This bronze trident, unearthed in central China, capped a high wooden post outside the leather tent of a nomadic chieftain. Made in the fourth century B.C., the three-pronged top is nearly five feet tall—a formidable emblem on the landscape.

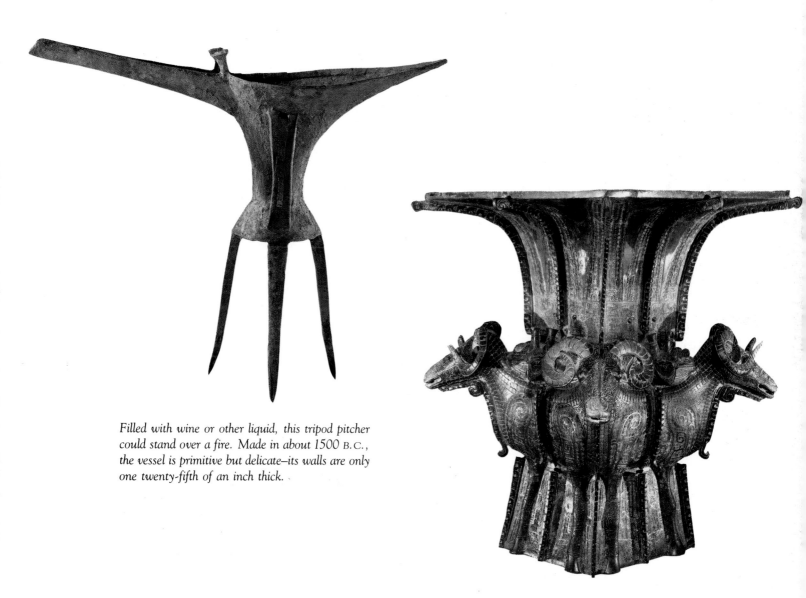

Filled with wine or other liquid, this tripod pitcher could stand over a fire. Made in about 1500 B.C., the vessel is primitive but delicate—its walls are only one twenty-fifth of an inch thick.

Stylized animal claws, horns, tails, and jaws twist around the elegant wine vessel (opposite). Cast between 1300 and 1030 B.C., the bronze urn is of a kind reserved for state officials.

Sentrylike rams guard the sacrificial contents of this bronze vase made in the eleventh century B.C. at a provincial foundry. The animals were an integral part of the original casting—only their horns and ears were added in a second stage.

OVERLEAF: In a detail of the vessel above, the seam dividing this ram's head results from the casting of symmetrical sections.

Age has not altered the original golden color of the beaker above, probably because of an abundance of copper in the bronze alloy. Made in the eleventh century B.C., the wine vessel bears a dedicatory inscription to a "Father Yi" and a clan emblem.

The massive caldron, opposite, was made in the mid-second century B.C. Except for the legs, the vessel was cast in a single pouring.

OVERLEAF: *A detail from a bronze caldron shows how the molten metal took the sculpted clay. The vessel belonged to Fu Hao, a Shang queen.*

II

CHINA'S FIRST EMPEROR

AND HIS HAN SUCCESSORS

Some time after 250 B.C., in the western state of Ch'in, a young king came to power. He was described by one of his officials as "a man with a high-bridged nose, long narrow eyes, the chest of a bird of prey, the voice of a jackal, and the mind of a tiger." Known as the Tiger of Ch'in, he was one day to become the first emperor of a united China, under the grandiose title Ch'in Shih Huang-ti, or First Supreme Emperor of Ch'in. Indeed the very name China is a simple derivative of Ch'in, whose first ruler was also the builder of the Great Wall, and the creator of numerous palaces where the imperial treasures might be displayed as evidence of his own riches and power–and these became evidence, too, of the continuously evolving glories of Chinese civilization.

All this was to be achieved at an appallingly heavy cost. But human life and suffering were not to be set in the scale against the glorification of a dynasty, the massive works of defense that would protect it from its enemies, and the splendid works of art

The ruthless Ch'in Shih Huang-ti, here riding through the countryside in a palanquin, unified China during his long reign.

that would proclaim its unparalleled culture. The Tiger of Ch'in and his successors in the Han dynasty would draw together a redoubtable state, developing its roads, its civil service, its trade, its defenses, training an elite to administer the state, setting up systems of patronage for artists and craftsmen. The nation they made has remained the greatest power in the Orient and one of the most advanced nations of the world.

The young king of Ch'in had great courage and energy, and a powerful will. The state he ruled covered roughly what are now the provinces of Kansu and Shensi in north central China. In the words of an ancient historian, "it was suspended thousands of feet above the rest of the empire. With twenty thousand men it could hold back a million spearmen." Ch'in was thus a formidable military power, whose mounted spearmen and archers with their siege trains of battering rams and scaling ladders thundered down upon their enemies, overwhelming them one by one.

In earlier times the people of Ch'in had scarcely been more than savage nomads. By the time of the Tiger of Ch'in, however, they had become economically as well as militarily successful; they had not lost their hardness and mercilessness in battle, but they had absorbed the culture of their conquered neighbors and had adopted many of their customs. In the third century B.C., a visiting Confucian philosopher praised their simple and natural demeanor, their sober clothing, their respect for precedent, and the authority of their "honest" and "worthy" officials. They seemed, indeed, a people destined for greatness.

At this same time an aspiring young man named Li Ssu, a disciple of the admiring Confucian traveler, turned his eyes hopefully toward Hsien-yang, the capital of this dynamic nation. Li Ssu had been born in Shang-ts'ai in the state of Ch'u in about 280 B.C. Although a devoted Confucian, he did not subscribe to all of his master's beliefs. He agreed that man acquired goodness only by training, but did not believe that the ideal feudal society could be achieved by precept. Li Ssu insisted men must be coerced and not be led. He was naturally drawn to the state of

Philosophy and history books blaze as Shih Huang-ti's henchmen cast Confucian scholars into a pit, in a detail from an eighteenth-century painting.

Ch'in, for there those philosophers known as Legalists were the dominant influence in government policy. They taught that men's actions were dictated by self-interest. A subject obeyed the law not out of reverence but out of fear.

Li Ssu soon came to the notice of the king of Ch'in's advisers, to whom he expressed his admiration for the way the king had subdued the feudal lords and had made Ch'in "the strongest state within the seas." The king made him senior scribe and later minister of justice. When in 221 B.C. the king proclaimed himself emperor of China, or Ch'in Shih Huang-ti, he asked his minister how his empire should be governed. Li Ssu replied that the empire must be divided into thirty-six provinces—each to be governed by men chosen for merit and loyalty. Meanwhile the leading families of the conquered territories must be brought to Hsien-yang where, deprived of power, they would devote themselves to the arts and scholarship.

Futhermore Li Ssu believed that the emperor ought to be exalted in every imaginable way. Huge armies of laborers, craftsmen, artists, smiths, and gardeners went to work not only on a splendid palace within the Imperial Park on the Wei River, but also on replicas of earlier palaces. As many as 700,000 prisoners and criminals, brought to Hsien-yang as forced laborers, built no less than 270 such palaces, filled with treasures, clustered around the city. They melted down bronze weapons and cast them into ornate bells and immense statues glorifying the First Emperor.

For his memorial near modern-day Sian he raised a vast tomb mound and in the shallow pits around the mound placed thousands of life-size pottery effigies of soldiers in uniform, of horses, and of war chariots. Excavations in 1975 revealed these figures in all their astonishing variety; and although the wooden chariots had rotted away except for their iron fittings, the statues of the soldiers, each one different from the next, are wonderfully preserved and their crossbows and bronze swords gleam as when the emperor's own troops held them. In 1981 at the same site, almost life-size figures of superbly rendered bronze came to light. These

TEXT CONTINUED ON PAGE 46

MONUMENTS TO POWER

The Tiger of Ch'in, who unified China in 221 B.C. and took the title Ch'in Shih Huang-ti, so feared death that he regularly left his palaces to search for the means to immortality: he consulted sorcerers, made sacrifices to any and all deities, foraged for allegedly magical fungi, and drank what he hoped were life-preserving elixirs. When the emperor died in 210 B.C., he was placed in an inner chamber behind a magnificent jade door, which remains sealed to this day. Crossbows were rigged throughout the underground mausoleum to slay vandals who might try to violate the innermost sanctum, where fabulous treasures were certainly buried.

Excavations of the emperor's "Spirit City," the area surrounding the still-unopened tomb, have brought to light the first evidence of what may be the most spectacular tomb in the history of the world. The Spirit City, a burial ground covering at least three acres, was built by 700,000 conscripted laborers (among them officials and scholars who had displeased the cruel king), and is populated with over 6,000 horses and armed warriors of clay, each of them an individual life-size portrait. The terra-cotta troops, once brightly painted, are cast as archers, cavalrymen, and charioteers. An army of equal size—this one made entirely of bronze and awaiting excavation—may guard another side of the vast tomb.

An archer, in an armored tunic and epaulettes, kneels to defend Shih Huang-ti's Spirit City.

In service to the First Emperor, clay charioteers, opposite, stand ready for their horses.

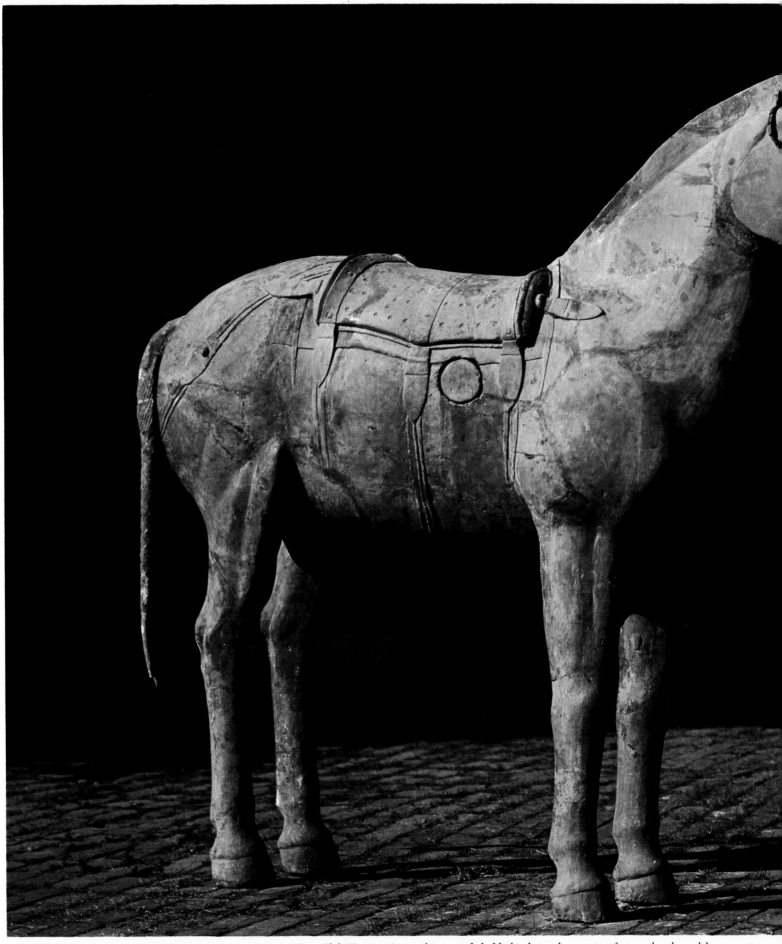

At rigid attention, a cavalryman from Shih Huang-ti's grandiose tomb holds his horse by a rein of stone beads and bronze wire.

Wearing ceremonial robes and bonnets, imperial officials of the Han dynasty confer in this drawing inspired by a tomb relief.

TEXT CONTINUED FROM PAGE 41

bronzes were part of a ceremonial procession–horses and chariots, each vehicle with its own pair of drivers, in bronze, one kneeling and the other standing–and they are the oldest ever found in China.

The First Emperor also built long, wide roads between plantations of trees, and had stone tablets inscribed with characters praising his virtues. And, so that no one would draw any unfavorable parallels between his own golden age and the past, Shih Huang-ti ordered that all books, save those "on medicine and pharmacy, divination...and the cultivation of land and trees," were to be burned. Scholars who disobeyed this order were tattooed on the cheeks or forced into chain gangs. Some authorities record that 460 recalcitrant scholars were buried alive in pits. Others were certainly sent to work on the Great Wall, then under construction as a defensive line against the barbarians in the north.

This immense fortification, Shih Huang-ti's greatest memorial, took about twelve years to complete and then it stretched some 1,400 miles–rising, dipping, curving, and looping across plain and mountain and river valley. Built of stone and brick and upon the material of earlier fortifications, rising sometimes to a height of fifty feet from a base twenty-five feet across, it was wide enough for eight men to march abreast along it between the garrison towers and watchtowers. It was a marvel of engineering; but it was, too, the graveyard of innumerable men and women who labored in suffocating heat or freezing cold to finish it. The dead and even the dying were interred in the wall as building material; perhaps as many as half a million people died while working on it, some of exhaustion in a merciless climate, others in attacks by the fierce tribes beyond the frontier, which were signaled by gongs and trumpets, fluttering flags, and smoke rising from piles of damp straw.

While the northern frontier was being secured, Shih Huang-ti sent expeditions to the south, expanding year by year the limits of his great empire. But he was growing old and his ambition was overcast by a consuming fear of death. He died at last in 210 B.C., a thousand miles from his capital on one of his many tours of his far-flung domains.

On this last tour he had brought along an ambitious and calculating eunuch, Chao Kao. Eunuchs were prominent in Ch'in Shih Huang-ti's court, as they had been in the royal court for centuries and would continue to be. Castration was a common state punishment for prisioners of war and lawbreakers; the eunuchs were the only males allowed inside the emperor's residence where the harem lived. In such close quarters with the emperor, they often rose to positions of power.

Chao Kao was hoping to rule the empire upon his master's death, and returned to Hsien-yang with the decaying imperial corpse, which was later buried with various slaves and favorite concubines in the huge—and still unexcavated—tomb near Lin-t'ung. The ambitious eunuch then made himself palace chamberlain. The new emperor's eldest brother committed suicide; twelve of his other brothers were executed; and the great minister, Li Ssu, was cut in half at the waist. The eunuch was now in full control of the government. However, the empire was being torn apart by rebels who found support among the discontented and overtaxed peasantry. They attacked the palace and soon afterward the eunuch was assassinated.

Out of this turmoil there emerged a rebel leader, Liu Pang, who was to establish a new dynasty. A peasant from east China, he was a rough, quick-tempered, shrewd, and likable man who "loved wine and women," according to the historian of his dynasty, and had "seventy-two black moles on his left thigh." Once a minor official, he became a bandit in the declining months of the Ch'in, then joined a rebel army that fell upon the splendid city of Hsien-yang, executed the successor emperor, and burned all the fine palaces to the ground. Liu Pang set up a new capital at Ch'ang-an, west of Loyang on the Yellow River, and there founded the dynasty that he chose to call Han, after a river in his homeland. It was to last for four hundred years, from 206 B.C. to

Tiny dogs at their feet, officials take their places on mats at a banquet in this scene from the same Han tomb as the one opposite.

Lutists make music for other ladies in their quarters. This scene and the ones on pages 49 and 50 are details from Spring Morning in the Han Palace, *a sixteenth-century scroll.*

A.D. 220, a mighty counterpart to the Roman Empire in the west, though in the arts, education, and even some aspects of government and warfare, more sophisticated than Rome. Even today the Chinese refer to themselves as "the sons of Han."

Liu Pang, who is better known by his posthumous imperial title, Kao-tsu, began to consolidate the imperial system of Ch'in Shih Huang-ti. The Han allowed the peasants more freedom and relieved them of the excessive taxes under which they had formerly labored; vassal kingdoms were permitted to re-emerge—but supervised by officials of the central government whose authority was absolute. The danger to the authority of the Han came not, in fact, so much from outside the palace as from within it. All was safe enough in the days of the hardheaded Kao-tsu; but in 195 B.C. he was mortally wounded in battle and was succeeded by a feeble son.

On the death of this weak emperor in 188 B.C., his mother, Empress Lü, placed an adopted son on the throne and, having had this child murdered, began to rule in her own right. She elevated members of her family to positions of influence and power; this grasping woman's relatives might almost have usurped the throne on her death. But, in fact, when she did die in 180 B.C., her late husband's followers massacred them all, placed one of his sons on the throne, and thus allowed for the accession in 141 B.C. of Emperor Wu-ti, "the Martial Emperor," in whose reign the Han led China in the kind of dynamic expansion characteristic of the great days of Ch'in.

Wu-ti was a practical man of limitless energy. He ruled personally, standing commandingly at the head of the empire's officials who, educated at an imperial university, themselves stood above and apart from ordinary people. He launched armies against the peoples of the south, conquering the modern provinces of Chekiang, Fukien, and the two Kwangs, and Vietnam. He brought the barbarians of Yünnan, Kweichow, and Szechuan under his dominion, and occupied Korea.

His immense forces of cavalry and infantry also poured north across the steppes and deserts to try and subdue the Hsiung-nu, those troublesome nomads beyond the Great Wall, known in the west as Huns. These warriors, who despised the weak and the old, learned horsemanship and archery as soon as they could walk. "They move on the feet of swift horses," a Han minister wrote, "and in their breasts beat the hearts of beasts. They shift from place to place as fast as a flock of birds...It would not be expedient to attack the Hsiung-nu. Better to make peace with them."

Wu-ti tried to make alliances against the Huns with the peoples of central Asia with whom he made contact. But he often felt compelled to resort to war, and army after army ventured north toward Shensi and the wastes of the Gobi in repeated efforts to subdue them. By about 100 B.C., indeed, Wu-ti's armies had penetrated farther from Ch'ang-an than even the legions of the Caesars had done from Rome, while his rule was recognized over a wider area than was that even of Augustus.

At the same time, the Chinese began to trade with the outside world. Caravans of handicrafts and bales of silk, whose manufacture remained a Chinese monopoly until the late sixth century A.D., moved in long lines to the west. Ivory, glass, linen, and wool came east in exchange, as well as gold, and more precious even than gold, herds of fine horses from central Asia —the celestial horses from the kingdom of Ferghana. The imperial family, the aristocracy, the landowners, the officials, and even the despised merchant classes grew rich and delighted in the display of their wealth.

Like the Shang and Chou treasures of an earlier epoch, the surviving Han dynasty treasures come chiefly from tombs. Comparatively few of them remain, but they are ample testimony to the sumptuousness of Han taste. There are paintings and maps on silk, fine lacquer ware, silk banners and robes, and finely wrought pieces of pottery and bronze, including some of the most beautiful bronze sculptures of horses ever made. And in one royal tomb, that of a Han prince buried in 113 B.C. and his prin-

Two maidens reclining amid fallen cherry blossoms read a book of verse. Their room, like others in the Han palace, opens onto the meticulously landscaped courtyard.

Servants tend a shrub planted with a t'ai-hu, a sculpted rock that the Chinese regarded as art and used in landscaping. Palace concubines and handmaidens shared duties in the Han garden.

cess, buried a few years later, are two of the most remarkable and luxurious items ever unearthed: two complete suits of resplendent jade. The larger of them contains 2,690 small jade chips, each perforated and stitched painstakingly with gold thread. And there were other riches as well—lamps, ritual vessels, sculptures, all of them literally matchless in the world of that day. If a young prince and princess could be buried in such magnificence, what must the emperor have owned?

Wu-ti was one of the last great Han emperors. His successors, less resolute than he, were constantly at violent odds with the families of the empresses and with the eunuchs of the court. And in A.D. 8 the nephew of an empress, Wang Mang, usurped the throne and established the Hsin, or New, dynasty. Unable to win the support of either the landlords or the peasants, Wang Mang did not last long. He was beheaded in his palace in A.D. 23 and soon afterward was succeeded by a descendant of the Han who restored the dynasty and established a new capital at Loyang, to the east of that destroyed by the rebels.

The first emperor of these later Han, Liu Hsiu, also called "the Shining Martial Emperor," was a strong and vigorous ruler as were his two immediate successors. But their successors were not. Unable to deal with the empire's worsening financial position, they could not even dominate the court, where the families of empresses and eunuchs grew more troublesome than ever. Beyond the painted walls further rebellions broke out. In east China the Yellow Turbans, led by Taoists who claimed magical powers, and in Szechuan other Taoist rebels, known as the Five Bushels of Rice—because that was the fee for initiation into the sect—rose up against the Han. The Han generals then turned against their masters; three of the most formidable split the empire up among themselves and thus began the period known as the Three Kingdoms. In the succeeding four hundred years there was constant warfare and unrest. Sometimes called the Period of Disunion, it was an age comparable to the one in Europe after the fall of Rome.

SPLENDORS OF
THE HAN

At peace in a funerary jacket of jade and gold, Han princess Tou Wan was laid to rest in a huge tomb furnished with the treasures she had most loved in life.

The imperial members of the prosperous Han dynasty surrounded themselves with luxury as no Chinese royalty had done before. And having lived in splendor, they took their treasures with them into the next world; intricately worked jade, lacquer ware, fine pottery, colored silks, and inlaid bronzes had their place first in palaces, then in tombs. On these and the following pages are a few of the beautiful things Han aristocrats chose to accompany them to their lavish graves. Horses were occasionally buried alive with Han kings, the fine steeds rigged to treasure-laden chariots of funeral corteges. Modeled on the legendary Ferghana horses of central Asia, the most prized of all breeds, Han equine bronzes inaugurated an enduring theme in Chinese art.

One of the most spectacular Han tombs was that of a prince, Liu Sheng, who consistently shunned politics for idle pleasures. When a brother criticized the way he "fritters away his days in sensual gratification instead of assisting the Son of Heaven," Liu Sheng answered, "A true king should pass his days...delighting himself with beautiful sights and sounds." The sybaritic prince did just that; when he died in 113 B.C. Liu Sheng was buried near Man-ch'eng in a tomb so opulent that it compared with the grandest of the pharaohs' in Egypt. Shrouded in jade and gold, Liu Sheng and his wife, Tou Wan (who died a few years after the prince), were buried with 2,800 of their treasures in a chamber dug out of solid rock by hundreds of slaves, and sealed with molten iron.

Nearly three thousand interlocking pieces of jade were individually cut, drilled, and sewn together with gold thread into Liu Sheng's burial suit, opposite. The Chinese believed that if all nine orifices were covered or filled with jade, the body would not decompose; the jade suit, an extravagant elaboration on that ritual, was unique to the Han dynasty.

Two dragons stand back to back atop this jade pi, *the ancient symbol of heaven, from Liu Sheng's underground mausoleum.*

53

Kneeling, her hair tied modestly back with a sash, a gilded girl (at left and in detail opposite) offers light to her mistress, Tou Wan, with whom the exquisite lamp was buried about 100 B.C. The princess, inside a jade suit similar to the one that encased her husband, Liu Sheng, lay next to the golden-faced sculpture, which held the lamp of "eternal fidelity."

Lying in serpentine coils, these leopards served as weights on the pall over Tou Wan's coffin. The cats, with their eyes of red garnet, were cast in bronze and decorated with gold and silver.

57

Tigers, deer, and hunters peer from the peaks of a fantasy mountain at the top of this bronze incense burner, which was placed near the body of Liu Sheng. The prince, like his contemporaries, believed that smoldering incense kept evil spirits at bay. The dark mountainous form (in detail at left) rises from swirls of gold inlay. Incense smoke coming through perforations would resemble mist rising from a mountain.

A hoof delicately placed on a stylized swallow, this galloping bronze horse becomes airborne. The sculpture was found with hundreds of other such figures in a second-century-A.D. tomb at Lei-t'ai in the northwestern province of Kansu.

OVERLEAF: From the same tomb as the horse at left, an Eastern Han official rides confidently in an escorted chariot. A man of rank and power, he is dwarfed by the canopy that signifies his authority. An abundance of horses and mounted men provided living symbols of power for the Han.

III

THE
GOLDEN AGE

OF THE T'ANG DYNASTY

The age that followed the Han was a time of division, sometimes of terror. Droughts, pestilence, and famine ravaged the countryside; the tempests raged and rivers burst their banks, inundating the fields and drowning whole communities. Towns lay in ruins, haunted by wild beasts and the specters of starving families. Hordes of nomadic horsemen constantly rode down from the steppes beyond the Great Wall in search of plunder and women, massacring tens of thousands of people and eventually occupying immense tracts of land. But these fierce invaders were at last obliged to seek the help of the old and experienced Chinese ruling caste in the territories they overran. Many of their leaders married daughters of Chinese aristocrats, and from one such marriage came Yang Chien, who was to establish a new dynasty, the Sui, and take the imperial name Wen-ti. This dynasty imposed order upon the devastated country and once again united north and south. And just as the Ch'in had prepared the way for the Han, so the Sui laid the founda-

T'ang emperor Ming-huang, reclining on a dais, turned from diligence to debauchery and in A.D. 756 finally abdicated to his serious-minded son.

tions of that great dynasty, the T'ang, rulers of the Chinese empire for almost three hundred years.

Wen-ti's successor, Yang-ti, one of the most powerful of the Sui, ruled from A.D. 605 to 618. He was a man of remarkable presence and dynamic energy. Relentless and ruthlessly ambitious, he cared as little for human life as had the tyrannical Ch'in Shih Huang-ti and sent as many men to die in the reconstruction of the Great Wall as Shih Huang-ti had sent to build it. Countless thousands of lives were also lost on laying out the new city of Loyang in the east and on building a network of canals between the valleys of the Yellow and Yangtze rivers. Of these the Grand Canal is the most remarkable; the cost and manpower that went into its construction have been compared to that involved in building the Great Wall. Between A.D. 605 and 610, tens of thousands of people were conscripted to complete this nine-hundred-mile waterway, which would connect north and south China for the first time. By means of all of these canals grain could travel from the "rice bowl" of the south through the north China plain to the garrisons guarding the frontiers.

And from time to time, down the canals, Yang-ti would set out with an enormous retinue of attendants, servants, and concubines on pleasure trips. He owned as many as forty thousand boats, and the royal barge was two hundred feet long and forty feet high with four decks. From the top deck the emperor could survey the seemingly endless procession of craft, which on one occasion was over sixty miles long. He could note with approval the willow trees planted by the banks, which were made of stone so that the wash of water did not wear them away. He could watch the soldiers pulling the boats along by ropes so that his passage would never be hindered by contrary winds. He could see caravans coming to town, among them cartloads of bird feathers with which court ladies adorned their dresses.

While thousands died in the construction of the canals, tens of thousands of men died, too, in military expeditions against the northern Koreans and other peoples. This megalomaniac

With the help of her handmaidens, Yang Kuei-fei, whom Ming-huang called his "Precious Consort," mounts a horse as the smitten emperor, on horseback, watches. The emperor, who was as devoted to the arts as to his favorite concubine, probably commissioned this painting.

disregard of human suffering as well as the drain upon the resources of the empire brought about the downfall of the dynasty less than thirty years after its foundation. But in those few years it had achieved so much in the reform of local and central administration and in the formation of a new legal code that the empire was regenerated. The next dynasty, T'ang, was to take most of the credit for all this accomplishment.

Under the T'ang a new golden age was to dawn in China. The central administration was restored. The government was ruled with firm authority but also with justice and tolerance. More splendid palaces filled with even finer trappings were built, towns were restored, and extensive canals were to be dug. New lands were seized from the surrounding barbarians and lost territories regained: Turkestan, Tibet, Korea, and Vietnam all came under Chinese influence or control. Meanwhile, the Arab raiders that had been encroaching on China's western lands were now held back behind the Hindu Kush mountains. Indeed, the civilization of China, which in Han times had been more advanced than any of the Mediterranean ones, was to become more powerful and sophisticated than they had ever been.

Like the Sui, the T'ang came from those half-nomad families of the north and, also like the Sui, their authority was constantly questioned by rich and ancient Chinese families, who looked down on them as usurpers. To counteract this challenge, the T'ang developed a system of state examinations that was eventually to create its own aristocracy, a bureaucratic elite. To pass these examinations, the candidate needed a classical, Confucian education. Consequently, the new ruling class was trained to apply ethical principles to the decisions they were required to make, to respect existing authority as well as traditional rituals.

The system naturally had its disadvantages: the curriculum was narrow and inhibited creative thought, and the stress on scholarship inclined to divide Chinese society quite as sharply as aristocratic birth had done. Yet the advantages of a civil service whose rewards were open only to men of talent, including studious and ambitious peasants, outweighed its drawbacks. The system may be one of the greatest Chinese achievements.

Quite as significant in the development of Chinese culture at this time was the spread of Buddhism. This universal religion, originating in India in the sixth century B.C., taught that the world is a transient reflection of the deity, that man's soul is a vital spark of this deity. Men and women are bound to suffer in this earthly life and the only way they can free themselves is to escape from consciousness and ultimately to reach Nirvana—a sinless state of mind achieved by the extinction of passion.

Buddhism, a crucially important link between the peoples of east and south Asia, was disseminated throughout China by pilgrims who had made the dangerous journey to India to study this religious philosophy in the country of its birth. It had inspired fine sculptures in the cave temples of Yün-kang and Lung-men, between the fourth and sixth centuries A.D., and Buddhist reliquary towers, which developed into pagodas. (The latter have always been one of the most distinctive architectural pleasures of the Chinese scene.) And it gathered countless thousands of adherents, including the early T'ang emperors. In A.D 645 the pilgrim monk Hsüan-tsang brought the Sanskrit scriptures back from India, and the emperors T'ai-tsung and Kao-tsung each wrote several prefaces for them.

In the reign of these two T'ang emperors—T'ai-tsung, who reigned from 626 to 649, and Kao-tsung, who died in 683—the ancient capital of Ch'ang-an was restored to a new glory. No achievement more dramatically symbolized the splendor of the T'ang than this magnificent metropolis, and the treasures it contained. It was the largest city in the world at that time; within its walls and suburbs and the immediate countryside lived almost two million people. The walls described a huge and precise rectangle six miles by five, covering an area about seven times as large as the modern city of Sian, which has succeeded it.

Twelve straight, wide, and exactly parallel roads ran from east to west, intersecting nine equally wide, straight thoroughfares

Having heard that a monk named Pien-ts'ai (seated in the armchair at left) had a beautiful calligraphy scroll, T'ang emperor T'ai-tsung sent an emissary (right) to steal it. This painting of the seventh-century escapade was made in about 1360.

running north to south. Travelers from the south would enter the city by the Great South Gate and, passing down the five-hundred-foot-wide central thoroughfare, would approach the Imperial City, where the government's offices and ministries stood in an enclave as perfectly rectangular as the city itself. On either side of them, toward the east and west ends of the eighth street the travelers crossed, were the two square government marketplaces. Beyond the Imperial City was the immense Imperial Palace and beyond that, outside the northern gate, was the Imperial Park. Each of the city's 112 blocks was a community of its own, locked up at night within its own walls, administered by its own officials, who were responsible to the central administration within the Imperial City. Ch'ang-an was, in fact, a microcosm of the empire of the T'ang, whose population of nearly fifty-three million people made it the largest state that the world had ever known.

The streets of the city were a scene of constant bustle, and in the workshops craftsmen of all kinds–smiths and jewelers, workers in jade and bronze, lacquer and glass, potters and tailors, wood carvers, silk weavers, furniture makers, seamstresses and masters of filigree–were laboring to produce those treasures prized by the imperial court both as beautiful objects in themselves and as evidence of the culture, the riches and the power of China, the center of the world, the fountainhead of civilization.

And the objects desired in the Imperial Palaces were desired, too, in the houses of the rich. So statues of jade and bronze dancing girls, athletes, and animals; looking glasses; pottery figurines and furnishings for tombs (to signify the worth of the departed and to recommend him to heaven); bas-reliefs of horses; silverwork and precious jewelry; gleaming bronzes; glazed bowls and vases–all poured forth from the hands of the craftsmen of Ch'ang-an and other T'ang cities in a seemingly endless stream.

No wonder that Ch'ang-an was a cultural and artistic magnet for the peoples of the outside world. Japanese missions came to China to study its art and culture: Kyoto was planned on the

TEXT CONTINUED ON PAGE 76

GRAVE GOODS OF BRILLIANT CLAY

Under the T'ang, China's most exuberant and affluent dynasty, vivid pottery sculptures were among the treasured accoutrements of royal and aristocratic burials—as bronze vessels had been over a thousand years earlier. Carefully molded of white clay, the finely detailed tomb figures were glazed in metal-based colors that imitated the brilliantly dyed textiles of the day. Servants, soldiers, loved ones, and prized horses were favored subjects; camels of clay attested to the deceased's interest in the exotic goods brought from India and the Near East by caravan. Standing in the recesses of burial chambers and lining the routes of grand funeral corteges, ferocious pottery guardians (such as the two on this page) protected the spirits of the dead.

This fierce genie from a tomb at Ch'ung-pu, near Sian in Shensi province, is trampling a demon.

This wild-eyed tomb guardian, above and in detail opposite, was made in the late seventh century, when T'ang potters had completely mastered their medium. Here, the colors run together, flowing down the figure and over the bull he stands on.

Saddled with fur blankets, their bridles hung with pendants and tassels, T'ang horses were evidence of power and prestige to the dynasty's rulers and privileged citizens. In addition to special trappings and grooming, some imperial horses also sported crenellated manes. The specimens here, realistically modeled and glazed with vibrant colors, are typical of the elaborately outfitted horses of the time. The figures come from tombs of T'ang noblemen.

73

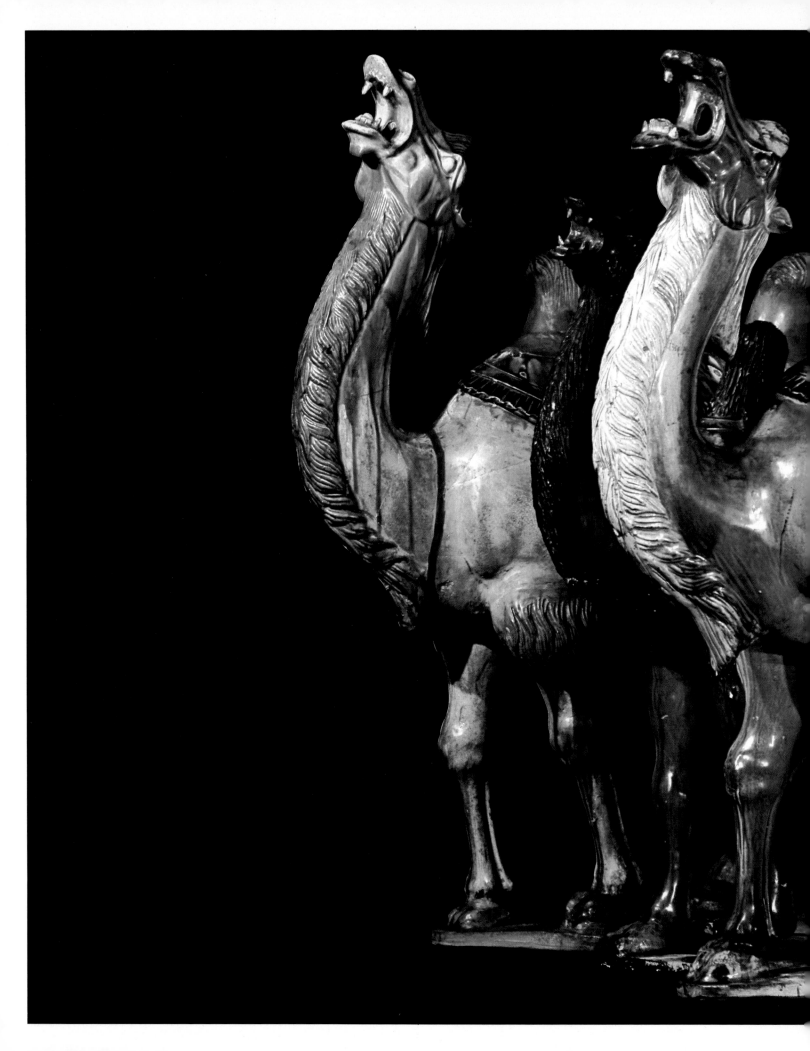

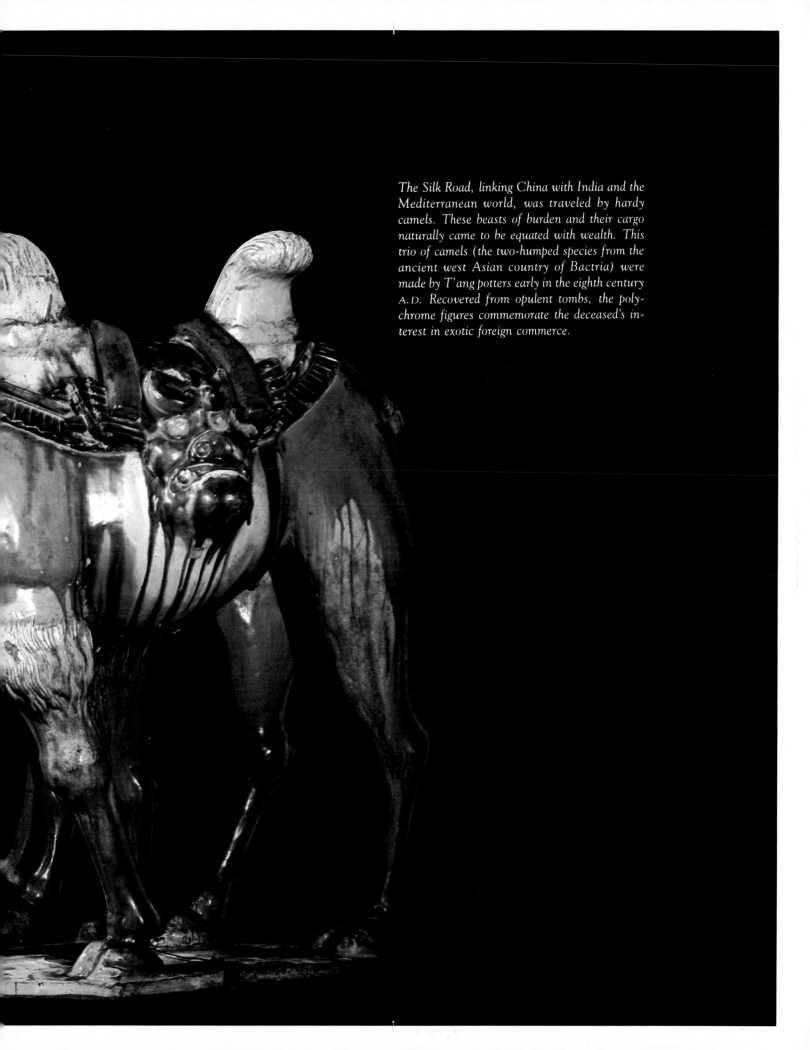

The Silk Road, linking China with India and the Mediterranean world, was traveled by hardy camels. These beasts of burden and their cargo naturally came to be equated with wealth. This trio of camels (the two-humped species from the ancient west Asian country of Bactria) were made by T'ang potters early in the eighth century A.D. Recovered from opulent tombs, the polychrome figures commemorate the deceased's interest in exotic foreign commerce.

TEXT CONTINUED FROM PAGE 69

lines of the splendid Chinese capital. Not only Japanese but merchants from all over Asia and Asia Minor came, and many of them settled, particularly in such southern ports as Yangchow and Canton. In Canton alone there were over 100,000 Jews, Muslims, and Persians. In Ch'ang-an there were residents of many nationalities, not only merchants but also diplomats and their retinues of officials and servants, monks and missionaries, scholars, writers, artists, and entertainers.

Visitors to China returned to their own countries with marvelous reports of the wonders of Ch'ang-an and other Chinese cities, of the efficacy of the T'ang system of government, and of the extraordinary inventiveness of the Chinese people. They had invented gunpowder—not for warfare but for the fireworks for which they still retain a passion. They had invented block printing and the wheelbarrow; they had long since been users of coal; they were expert in the manufacture of paper and ceramics; they were as skillful at cartography as calligraphy.

The influence of China on the outside world was, however, matched by the outside world's influence on China. From India, for instance, came a deeper knowledge of astronomy and traditions in the plastic arts, particularly in sculpture, which were to revolutionize those arts in China. Many Buddhist images, heads, reliefs, and statues produced under the T'ang are strongly reminiscent of those carved in India.

As patrons of artists and poets and such Buddhist scholars as Hsüan-tsang, both the emperors, T'ai-tsung and Kao-tsung, could take much credit for the flowering of Chinese culture. So could Empress Wu, one of the most remarkable women in the whole of Chinese history. She had been a concubine in the seraglio of Kao-tsung's father. Here Kao-tsung had seen her and after his father's death, had claimed her and raised her to imperial rank. Her beauty, lasciviousness, and cruelty soon became notorious. She had two of her chief rivals in the emperor's affections executed by having their feet and hands chopped off and their maimed bodies placed in tubs of spirits, where they died

Attendants of the T'ang princess Yung-t'ai carry gifts for their mistress: silks, candles, cosmetics, a fan, and a back scratcher. She died in the late seventh century A.D. *at the age of nineteen —perhaps at the hands of her own grandmother, Empress Wu. This detail is from a mural in the anteroom of the princess' tomb.*

slowly. After the death of her husband, she ruled the empire through two of her sons, clothing herself in the robes of the sovereign and abolishing the ancestral temples of the T'ang.

In 690, having ruthlessly exterminated all opposition, she took the unprecedented step for a woman of ruling China in her own name. For fifteen years she ruled ably until she herself was removed in a coup. Her son and successor was then overthrown by his own empress. She would have followed Empress Wu's example by ruling in her own name, had not these palace revolutions been brought to an end after Ming-huang, Empress Wu's grandson, took the throne to begin his forty-five-year reign in 712.

He began in triumph but was to end in tragedy. For although Ming-huang commenced his rule as a young and vigorous man, learned and politically astute, with an apparently stable empire, portents of trouble were obvious. The population was still increasing; so were the empire's riches. But the expenses of public works, defense, the complex bureaucracy, and the imperial court had also increased. The peasants, who were required to serve in the militia at their own expense, could no longer do so: they deserted in large numbers. The T'ang had to rely on expensive mercenaries. Defeat followed military defeat until in 751 Chinese armies were routed both in the southwest and, more crucially, in the far west, beyond the mountains of central Asia. The Arabs, long held at bay, won a fateful victory here, foreshadowing the end of Chinese mastery of that important area.

Depressed by defeats along his frontiers and by frequent quarrels between the old aristocracy and the new bureaucracy, the emperor sought escape from his troubles in Taoist mysticism and the luxurious pleasures of his court. His harem was said to contain forty thousand concubines. He had several hundred of his women taught to play musical instruments in the Pear Garden of the Imperial Park; and he spent hours on end in the company of Yang Kuei-fei, a beautiful concubine whom he took from the harem of his son, giving him another girl in exchange. He spent hours, too, planning court festivities, for which he commis-

Outnumbered and unarmed but victorious, General Kuo Tzu-i offers peace to the cowering leader of a tribe that in A.D. 765 had invaded the T'ang capital of Ch'ang-an. This scene is from an eleventh-century handscroll.

sioned suitable poems from the court poets he patronized.

As time passed the emperor grew ever more helplessly in love with the entrancing Yang Kuei-fei and could deny her nothing. Litchis were her favorite fruit: horsemen were, therefore, kept constantly galloping along the fifteen hundred miles of road between Canton and Ch'ang-an so that she would always have a fresh supply. The emperor ennobled her father and all three of her sisters, and appointed her brother a principal minister at court. As well as the members of Yang Kuei-fei's family, Minghuang promoted and indulged all her friends. One of these was a rough and rowdy young general, An Lu-shan, whom she was said to have taken as her lover.

An Lu-shan hated Yang Kuei-fei's brother and was jealous of his power. He also despised the idle, aging emperor, and he determined to raise a rebellion to overthrow them both. As commander of more than 150,000 troops on the northeastern frontier, he was well placed to do so. Overwhelming the troops that were sent against him, the rebel general occupied Loyang and marched upon Ch'ang-an. Advised to flee to Szechuan, the emperor and his party left without provisions of any kind.

Two days later, at a place called Ma-wei, his soldiers, hungry, tired, and mutinous, turned upon their masters. They cut Yang Kuei-fei's brother to pieces and demanded that Yang Kuei-fei be executed, too. So, with evident horror, he issued the order for his beloved concubine's death. Some reports say that Yang Kuei-fei hanged herself in a tree; others that she was dragged into a nearby Buddhist temple and strangled.

Inconsolable, the emperor spent the rest of his life "washing his face with a fountain of tears." He abdicated in favor of his son who, while An Lu-shan's troops were looting Ch'ang-an, was able to gather his forces and save the dynasty until 907. Yet the great days of the T'ang were now over forever. The last of the T'ang emperors tended to be debauchees and wastrels, governed by the women and eunuchs of the palace. Another cycle in the imperial history of China was closed.

AN ACQUIRED TASTE

Flowering vines of gold cover a tiny silver box in the form of a ram, with gilded head and hooves. The T'ang elite coveted the precious metals as no Chinese had before.

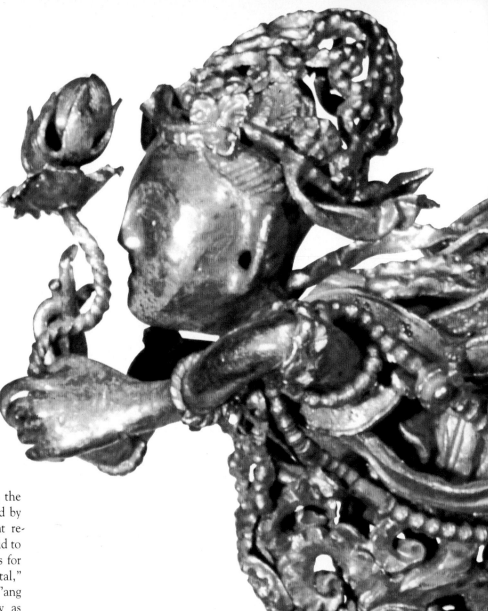

Unlike most other peoples of the world, the Chinese were not immediately dazzled by gold and silver, nor did they attach great religious significance to the metals, as they did to jade and bronze. The T'ang had no words for the elements: gold was simply "yellow metal," silver was "white metal." But during the T'ang dynasty, gold and silver, once used only as currency or as trimming for bronze and jade, came into their own as treasures.

The precious metals were not easy to find. To supplement their meager livings, farmers labored in state silver mines and searched rocks and rivers for gold, grateful even for grains so small they were called "wheat bran." At the cosmopolitan capital of Ch'ang-an and other cities, smiths worked the gold and silver into extravagant jewelry and utensils. T'ang metalsmiths were peerless in their technical mastery, whether beating out foil, tracing decoration into hammered sheet metal, or making filigree, repoussé relief, and beading. Yet people looked upon goldsmiths and silversmiths as craftsmen, not artists, and did not grant them the high status of painters or calligraphers; nevertheless, their creations made the time of the T'ang dynasty a true Golden Age.

A golden apsara—the Buddhist angel—floats on a cloud, holding high the symbol of the doctrine, a sacred lotus blossom. The angel, made in the eighth century, trails ribbons, scarves, streamers, and beads, all of soldered gold. One of a pair, it was probably part of an elaborate T'ang altar set.

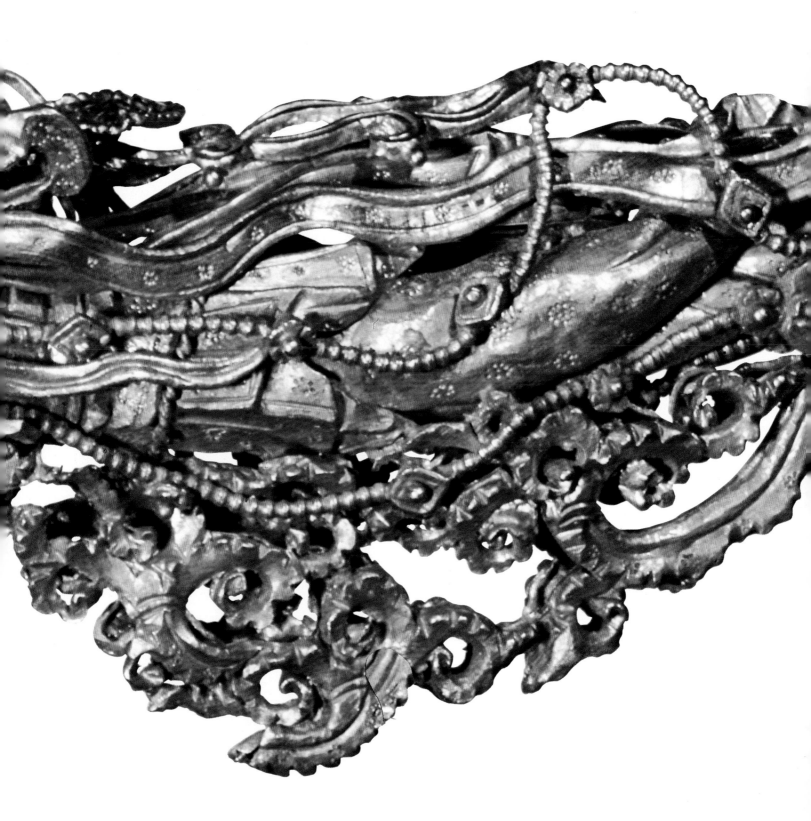

A lady of the late T'ang imperial court wore—and was buried with—this headdress of golden branches and blossoms. Rubies, pearls, and cat's-eyes hang from the filigree of pure gold.

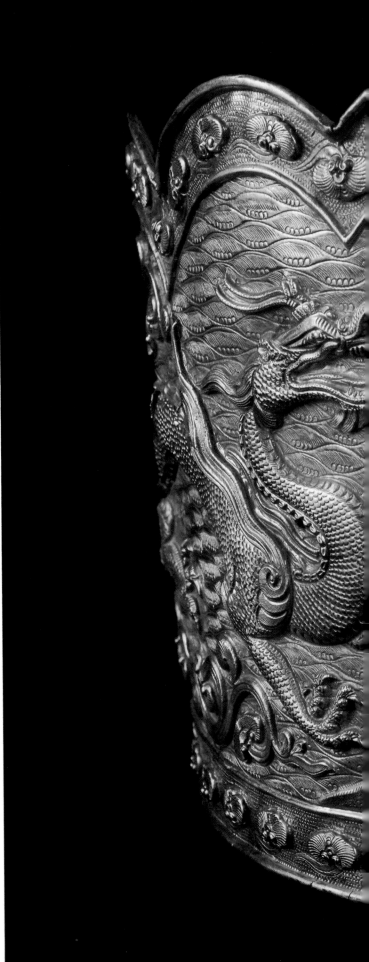

Two dragons pursue a ball of fire in the center of this crown of gilded silver. The entire surface decoration is repoussé, i.e., raised from the backside of the metal. The crown was presented to an official envoy to the Chinese court late in the tenth century.

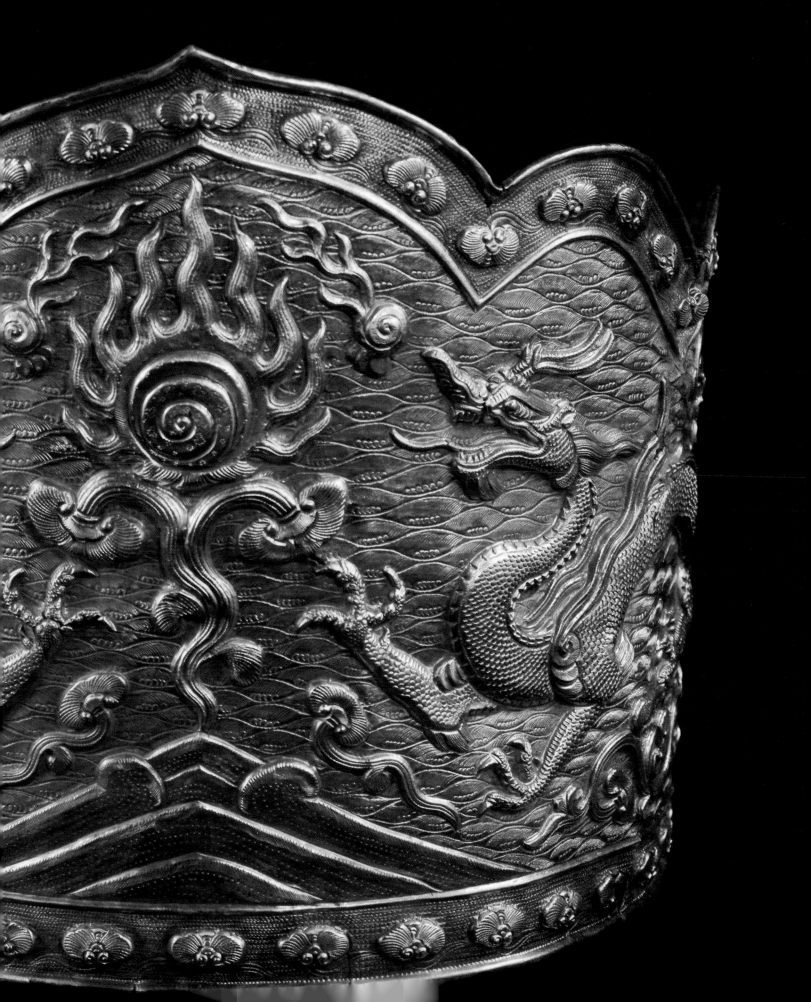

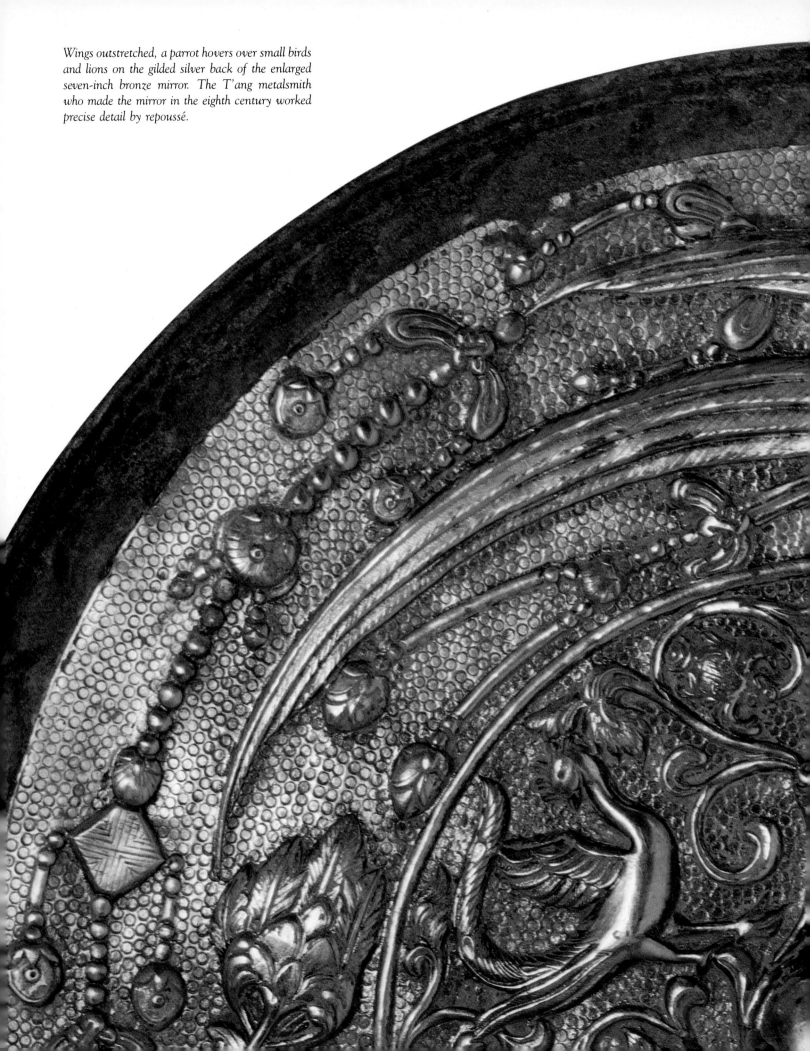

Wings outstretched, a parrot hovers over small birds and lions on the gilded silver back of the enlarged seven-inch bronze mirror. The T'ang metalsmith who made the mirror in the eighth century worked precise detail by repoussé.

The first Buddhist sculptures in China, celebrating the religion born in India, were carved into rocky cliffs along the Silk Road, the route of the pilgrims as well as merchants. The sobriety and discipline required of Buddha's devotees at first resulted in rigid icons; by the sixth century A.D., these images had become fluid and graceful, as seen in the three sculptures below. The fluidity of form came in part from a medium which was more malleable than stone: T'ang artists produced bronze sculptures, molding the figures in clay, casting them in molten metal, and gilding the finished pieces.

CELESTIAL DANCER, GILDED BRONZE, EIGHTH CENTURY

GUARDIAN DEITY, C. SEVENTH CENTURY

GILDED BRONZE BUDDHA FROM EARLY EIGHTH CENTURY

OVERLEAF: *In a detail from the bronze above, the Buddha's hands indicate that he is about to preach on the liberation of the spirit from worldly passions.*

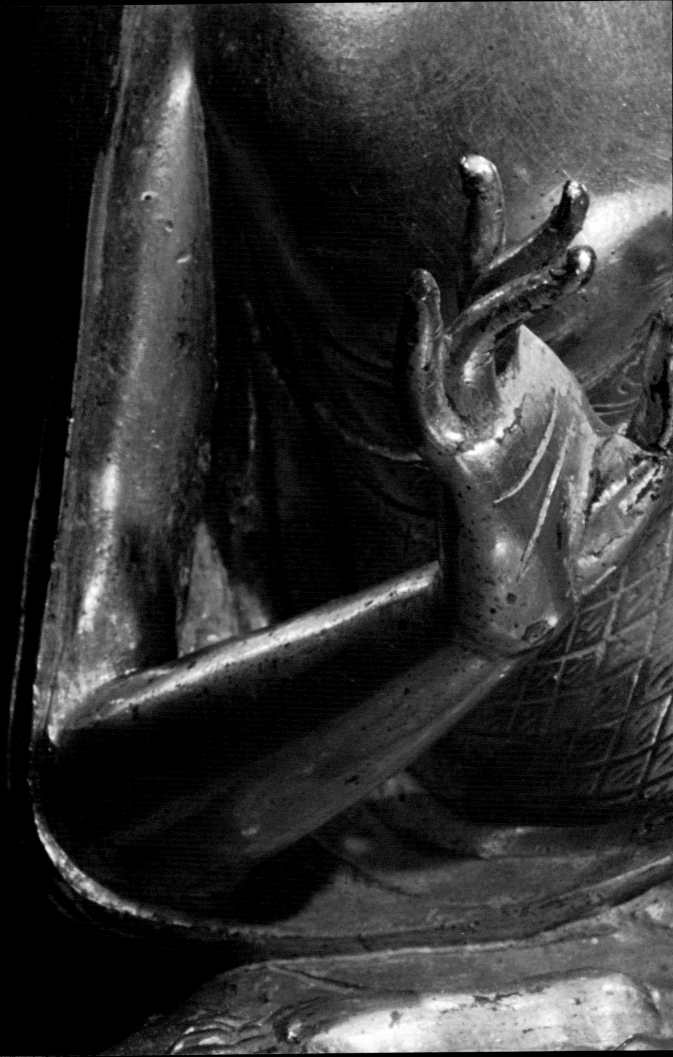

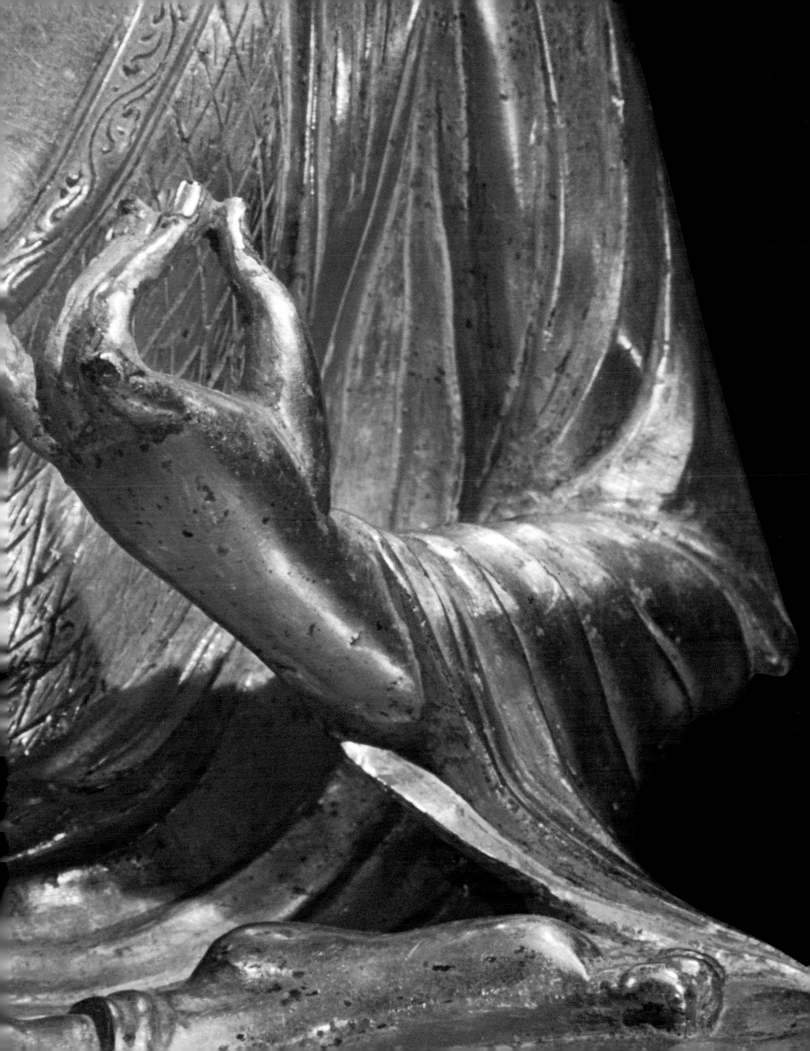

IV

THE POET-EMPEROR

OF THE SUNG

As at other times when the Chinese empire was on the verge of collapse, a strong man now came to power. This was Chao K'uang-yin, a young general who had defeated many of the provincial warlords and who had caught the notice of the last dying T'ang emperor not only as a successful soldier but also as a scholar.

Early in 960 the emperor put Chao K'uang-yin in charge of a large expeditionary force against the troublesome Khitan Tartars of Inner Mongolia. One evening early in the march, having retired to bed in an inn, the commander was awakened by loud shouts and the clash of arms. He leaped to his feet and opened the window. The courtyard was filled with his soldiers, both officers and men, waving their swords and calling out his name. When he appeared, a group of senior officers cried out, "Commander! Be our Emperor! Emperor of China!" One of them went into the inn and placed a robe of imperial yellow around the general's shoulders; and at this the soldiers all knelt down before

The emperor Hui-tsung, a poet and a painter, was the most refined of art connoisseurs but a naive ruler whose reign brought catastrophe to China.

him, calling out "Long live the Emperor!" Later they rode back with him to Kaifeng where the crown prince, who had inherited the throne after his father's death, promptly abdicated. The general took the imperial title; and as Emperor T'ai-tsu, he founded the Sung dynasty, which was to last for over three hundred years.

T'ai-tsu was an unassuming man, considerate toward his subordinates and merciful in his dealings with rivals and enemies. At the same time he was both ambitious and astute. Mindful of how he had come to power, he was determined not to lose that power in the same way. So he invited all the leading military commanders to a banquet at the Imperial Palace; and there, having eaten and drunk well with them, he declared, "If it had not been for you, my generals, I should never have become emperor. I have sleepless nights, worrying about the power that you all possess. Now what I propose is that you should all resign your military appointments. I will give you positions where you can make money and buy lands to leave to your children, and in the meantime you can enjoy life to the full. Any man willing to accept my proposal will be treated as my friend and our families will intermarry."

Either tempted by his proposals or afraid to reject them, all the generals resigned the next day. Thus T'ai-tsu was able to remove the greatest threat to his dynasty, to check the power of local military commanders, and to bring the army under central, civilian control. Henceforth he appointed only civil officials as governors, and made these officials directly responsible to himself. As his representatives, they lived in their own provinces to validate the governor's rulings and to supervise the collection of taxes. Meanwhile, the emperor moved senior officers from one command to another to keep them from gaining too much influence. Military units, too, were posted periodically from one garrison to the next so that the soldiers would think of themselves as the emperor's men. Finally, upon the advice of his strong-willed mother, T'ai-tsu decreed that after his death the imperial title should pass to his brothers rather than to his sons so that the

Scholars meet in a garden for food and talk in Hui-tsung's painting A Literary Gathering. *The garden was the one place where strict court protocol was suspended and the emperor could mingle with scholars to paint their portraits.*

Sung might have the undoubted benefit of mature leadership.

Thus the Sung were soon established in authority, and the empire reunited. The imperial court could once more devote itself to the pleasures of civilized life. No emperor took keener and more aesthetic delight in such pleasures than Hui-tsung, the "Imperial Dreamer," who came to the throne in 1101, more than a century after T'ai-t'su's death. A highly gifted poet, a leading painter of the day, an antiquarian and archaeologist, he was also an avid collector with an affinity for rare pieces, particularly of porcelain, whose makers reached new heights of artistry in his time. He had a special museum built to house his collections, which he constantly augmented with gifts from people who wished to gain his favor and with acquisitions from others whom he bullied into parting with their valued possessions.

Hui-tsung spent so much time, indeed, inspecting his acquisitions, writing poetry, painting, supervising the erection of temples, attending religious ceremonies, and making love to a celebrated courtesan that he had little time to spare—and less inclination—for the affairs of the empire. Yet political problems were becoming ever more pressing, for the Sung empire at this time had gradually begun to shrink in size as its enemies encroached upon its frontiers. A previous emperor, T'ai-tsung, had been forced to come to terms with the Khitan Tartars and to pay a large annual subsidy. And in 1125 Hui-tsung was driven into a costly war with the fierce nomadic Nüchen Tartars, former vassals of the Khitans, who had become masters of northeast Asia.

In 1126 the Nüchen warriors rode into the Sung capital, Kai-feng, in the Yellow River valley, and took three thousand men into captivity, including the emperor himself. He was forced to appear before the Nüchen leader in the blue robes commonly worn by servants. His captors addressed him sardonically as the Duke of Confused Virtues and sent him away beyond the Great Wall, where he died. The Nüchen then advanced south and came so close to capturing the Sung city of Hangchow that Hui-tsung's successor, Emperor Kao-tsung, made an alliance with

them. The pact left the Nüchen to control the north on condi-
tion that the Sung were left in peace in the rice-growing valleys
of the south.

By this time, despite these upheavals, China had entered yet
another golden age. Sung achievements in science and the arts,
and in the development of social institutions, eclipsed even
those of the T'ang. New towns sprang up all over the empire. In
the north no less than thirty-six provincial capitals and several
hundred small towns and administrative centers grew around the
capital of Kaifeng. These model towns were uniform—walled cities with three gates on all four sides studded with tall towers and
often surrounded by moats. The houses of the senior officials
were in the center, the temples to the south, the markets to the
north. The pattern was, however, less regular in the beautiful
city of Hangchow, which the emperor Kao-tsung had established
as the Southern Sung capital in 1135. There was, in fact, a variety and liveliness about life in Hangchow that enchanted every
visitor.

At its height, the city covered eight square miles, the city
proper being circumscribed by thirty-foot, crenellated walls of
whitewashed earth and stone. A straight, wide thoroughfare
known as the Imperial Way ran north to south; the main canals
ran parallel to it; other streets crossed it east to west. All the
main streets were paved with stones and bricks, well graveled in
the middle, drained by conduits that took the rainwater into the
canals, and regularly swept. From early in the morning—when
the bells of the Buddhist and Taoist monasteries rang, and
monks walked through the streets beating strips of iron to an-
nounce the dawn—until daybreak the following day these streets
and canals were scenes of constant activity. Boats laden with rice
and wine, with firewood and sacks of salt and fresh vegetables,
passed northward through the city and down to the river, where
innumerable barges, fishing boats, and junks with sails of pleated
matting were anchored beneath the green mountains.

The streets were filled with porters carrying goods suspended

*In 1070 the minister Ssu-ma Kuang retired from
office in a policy dispute and spent the next fifteen
years writing history. In this painting he takes refuge
from the heat in a bamboo grove, part of his
Garden of Solitary Enjoyment.*

from long poles or chairs with canopies and folding doors. Inside these sat ladies clothed in silks and gold brocade, or in quilted, fur-lined coats in the colder weather, with pins and combs in their neatly arranged and shining black hair, their skin dusted with a deep rose shade of powder and their nails painted pink. Others sat in carriages fitted with curtains and cushions, their men riding horses beside them. Despite such indulgences, however, women in general were repressed even more severely under the Sung. A tiny, misshapen foot, the result of the practice of foot-binding, came to be a sign of wealth—who but a rich man could afford to keep handicapped wives and daughters? And so, for centuries, the foot bones of young female children were painfully crushed, and the feet tightly bound.

On either side of the crowded streets rose the houses, of wood and bamboo and partly of brick, some five stories high. They were all "well built and elaborately finished," wrote one admiring visitor. "The people's delight in decorating, in painting and architecture leads them to spend such sums of money as would astonish you." The poorer houses were thatched, but those of the more well-to-do were curved and covered with yellow and green glazed tiles, their exposed beams carved and painted and often decorated with terra-cotta animals and dragons. The richest lived in beautiful houses built around a series of courtyards and gardens where rare flowers grew between mounds of veined and polished stones.

The emperor's palace was the most magnificent of all. Its pavilions were ornamented with gold, its walls painted with delicate representations of the triumphs of his ancestors. In the extensive gardens were artificial hills planted with pines and bamboos; waterfalls splashing their waters into lakes where lotuses and water lilies spread their leaves over the sparkling water; enclosures where all manner of animals roamed and birds of the brightest plumage flew from tree to tree; courtyards in which orchids, jasmine, and cinnamon blossomed in urns, and their scents wafted through the windows of the emperor's rooms.

TEXT CONTINUED ON PAGE 104

THE SOUL OF LUXURY

In their grace of form and subtlety of color, Sung stoneware and porcelain are the most beautiful the world has seen. The examples on these pages represent the culmination of millennia of artistic and technical experimentation in ceramics—an art for which the Chinese possessed a unique talent. Although it was the blue and white porcelain of the later, Ming period that became famous in the West, the Chinese have always regarded Sung porcelain as the best. As early as 1100 B.C. Chinese potters created stoneware, a type of pottery shiny in appearance, so hard a knife could not scratch it, and resonant—when tapped with a finger it sounded a musical tone. The ultimate refinement of stoneware is translucent white porcelain—a Chinese invention of the seventh century A.D. The Chinese guarded their techniques more closely than they kept the secret of silk. It was not until the early 1700s that Europeans, after a century of trying, were able to make their own porcelain.

By altering the proportions and types of metal, such as lead or iron, that went into the glaze of a piece, potters produced a wide variety of color effects, some with evocative names—"moonlight" ware of lavender-blue with streaks of purple, and "partridge feathers" ware of maroon or sienna with flecks of a light color. At the Northern Sung court, where moderation was considered the soul of luxury, restrained Ting porcelain of plain ivory color (see page 102) was fashionable until Hui-tsung banned it because of blemishes, or "tear drops," in the glaze. He preferred opalescent blue Ju stoneware (below and opposite). Reserved exclusively for the palace and made only during Hui-tsung's reign, Ju ware is among the rarest and most precious Sung art objects; only fifty-three pieces survive today.

Blue-green with delicate touches of pink, the Ju ware bowl above epitomizes the subtle colorations achieved by Sung potters.

The voluptuous, curving shape of this Ju ware vase is typical of the forms admired by the refined Sung connoisseurs.

The soft color of this incense burner, a blend of grey, blue, and green that resembles jade, is characteristic of Lung-ch'üan ware—highly prized throughout Asia from the Sung period onward. Indian and Middle Eastern rulers purchased Lung-ch'üan pieces for their households because they believed the ware possessed the magical power to reveal the presence of poison in food.

The maker of this vase artfully incised it to resemble a fish basket fashioned from willow plaits, adding the realistic detail of a cord knotted at the neck. The fine ivory color and metal lip are marks of Ting porcelain.

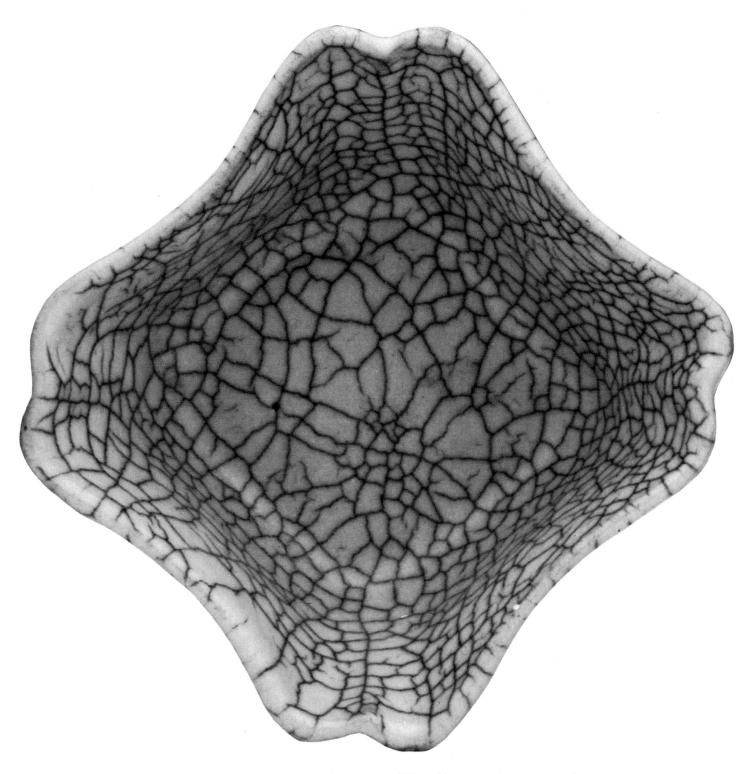

The dark lines in the glaze of this cup are called crackle. Originally potters considered crackle an imperfection, until they realized the decorative possibilities of these fine lines and began using them in a variety of patterns.

TEXT CONTINUED FROM PAGE 97

The furniture in these rooms was simple but decorative. There were small tables and armchairs, beds enclosed by painted screens and covered with silk, circular stools set against the walls upon which hung scrolls depicting country scenes. Red lacquer was the dominant form of decoration.

Every rich man's house had its bathroom; and the ordinary people, too, enjoyed the pleasures of bathing, for there were public baths in every quarter of Hangchow. There were tea-houses, too, where both tea and wine were served in little porcelain cups, where rich merchants and officials came to learn music, and where, in the upper rooms of many such establishments, singing girls were to be found. There were pleasure grounds where plays were acted; there were gaily painted boats for trips to be taken on the lake; there were pretty prostitutes, both male and female, in the arcades of the taverns.

Another pleasure for the rich was food, prepared and served with the unique artistry that had become a hallmark of Chinese culture. The most common dishes were rice, pork, vegetables, and salted fish. But rabbits and geese, venison and mutton, quails and duck, shrimps and partridges, were all to be found in abundance in the markets. In the numerous restaurants every kind of dish was on the menu, from silkworm pies to birds' nest soup. Much of the food, including fish, was served iced; but the wine was nearly always warm, and people consumed a great deal of it. Drunkenness was common: the canals had to be balustraded because so many revelers fell in.

Relatively few could enjoy life, of course. For the poor, life was hard and the working day long. There was work enough for skilled men to do in the immense variety of crafts, but for the untrained peasants, who now flocked to the towns in great numbers, it was not always easy to find work. They might find jobs as sweepers or water carriers or road menders or scavengers, but many became thieves or beggars.

Yet, if poverty and squalor were everywhere, so too was the evidence of a civilization far in advance of any in the West. In

A woman irons silk in a detail from a scroll by Hui-tsung. Though the emperor copied the scene from another artist's painting, Hui-tsung's skillful composition, brush strokes, and use of color have made this work famous in its own right.

every large town in Sung China there were signs of the great advances that were being made in science and technology. In Kaifeng, for example, was a huge astronomical clock of astonishing complexity. Elsewhere there were water mills grinding corn by intricate systems of interconnecting cogs, and workshops that used water power for spinning hemp. On the rivers, locks and bridges demonstrated the ingenuity of Chinese engineers, while off the coast there were ships with multiple masts and treadmill-operated paddles. The magnetic compass had already been perfected by the tenth century. A manned calculating device called the abacus gained widespread use in late Sung years and has remained the primary instrument of computation for east Asian merchants ever since. Great advances were being made, too, in the study of medicine and zoology, mathematics and algebra, history and geography. Chinese agriculture was the most productive in the world. Publishing centers flourished by the eleventh century, following the invention of movable type.

There were simultaneous developments in the arts. Painters produced those beautiful misty landscapes and delicate pictures of birds and flowers that are among the finest treasures of the Eastern world. Emperor Hui-tsung was himself a highly talented artist and patron. He established an imperial institute of calligraphy and painting and supervised the compilation of a catalog with 6,396 paintings by 231 artists. Skill in painting, like expert calligraphy and facility in the composition of verse, became an important factor in passing the civil service examinations.

Emperor Shen-tsung's minister Wang An-Shih, "the Bull-Headed Premier," a man who never noticed what he was eating or cared what clothes he wore, who pushed through a series of economic, educational, and military reforms, was also a poet and celebrated prose stylist. Another high official named Su Tung-p'o acquired an eclectic reputation as a painter and calligrapher, an experimenter in wine-making and alchemy, a practicer of yoga, an intriguing conversationalist, and one of China's greatest poets and essayists. When serving as governor of Hang-

A poet, having drained his bowl of wine, weighs the words of a poem in his mind before putting them on paper. He sits beneath a curving willow—a symbol of sensual elegance meant to reflect the poet's mood of creative intoxication.

chow, he once was asked to deal with a fan merchant who had been arrested for debt. The merchant explained that he was in debt because no one wanted to buy fans. Su Tung-p'o then told the man to bring him a bundle of his fans. The governor spent an hour or two decorating them with scripts and lovely pictures of bare winter trees and summer bamboos. Then he handed the fans to the merchant and said, "Go and pay your debts."

Neither civilized governors such as Su Tung-p'o, however, nor civilization itself did much to ameliorate the hardships of the ordinary peasants' lot. In the summer they remained in the fields all day; in the winter they were put to work building the towns. There were always animals to feed, silkworms to raise, winnowing and weaving to do, buildings to repair. According to an account of that time:

The man is hired for the season, generally from the first moon [February] until the ninth [October]. His wage is one "load" [about 8 bushels] of cereals per month. His employer undertakes to furnish him with free clothing, a "spring" outfit, a shirt and trousers for summer, and a pair of leather shoes. In exchange he must work without stopping, from morning until evening... If he falls ill, payment for the days when he is not at work, is deducted from his wages. If he loses or damages the agricultural goods entrusted to him, he has to see that they are replaced.

As peasant discontent grew toward the end of the thirteenth century, so did the threat from the empire's foreign enemies. The Mongol hordes of a ruthless, brilliant chieftain named Genghis Khan poured over the Great Wall and by 1227, when Genghis died, had become masters of most of northern China. A few years later they began to move farther south. The Sung armies were the best in the world. Gunpowder was now a weapon, and the Mongols had to face explosive bombs and grenades as well as rockets, flame throwers, and poisonous smokes. But the Sung soldiers were no match for the hardy tribesmen of the steppes. In 1279 the last surviving Sung prince died just before the start of a naval battle in the South China Sea and Genghis' grandson Kublai Khan became emperor of all China.

THE REALM OF
THE SPIRIT

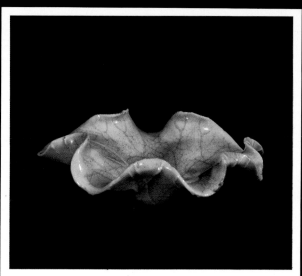

A Sung artist used this porcelain brush washer, in a delicate
lotus-leaf shape with realistic veins below its surface, to clean
his brushes after writing or painting.

"I n my moments of leisure from the innumerable affairs of state I seek no other pleasure than painting," remarked Hui-tsung to his ministers. Indeed painting preoccupied the emperor, who created and otherwise acquired an enormous collection of more than six thousand works, including most of the landscapes on these pages. By Hui-tsung's reign (1101 to 1125), landscape painting had long been the premier Chinese art form. Mountains were the preeminent theme of the genre: the Sung landscapists rendered monumental mountain scenes—sometimes seven feet high—of jagged granite peaks split by waterfalls and cloaked in mist. The Chinese artists' fascination with mountains goes back to the origins of landscape painting in the fourth century A.D., when mountains were believed to be magical places where spirits dwelled. In succeeding centuries "mountain and water painting," as the Chinese referred to landscape art, kept its magical associations and also became intimately linked to philosophy—to both rational Confucianism and mystical Taoism. For example, the stature of humans in a landscape painting reflects the Taoist concept of man as a diminutive creature, dwarfed by the vastness and complexity of nature. Confucian thinkers, for their part, held that a landscape painting can reveal the governing order of the universe, which is intact in nature but imperfect in man. In their effort to convey the order and unity of nature, Chinese artists virtually abandoned the use of color in favor of the austere, demanding medium of ink on silk—a medium closely related to calligraphy. This simple technique became powerfully expressive in the hands of masters such as Li Ch'eng (active from 940 to 967) and Fan K'uan (990 to 1030), whose works exemplify a Taoist view of landscapes: "they exist in material substance and soar into the realm of the spirit."

The meticulous architecture of a temple contrasts with the wild landscape of writhing trees and jagged cliffs in Buddhist Temple in the Hills After Rain. *The scroll has been attributed to the master landscape painter Li Ch'eng, but may be a copy. The collection of Hui-tsung included 159 of Li Ch'eng's landscapes.*

似霞醉露零庭爛萼依穠
融照殘如露中一煥翠芳

晚翩徑迷舞留化筆難丹
風逐翩香蝶工獨造下青

HUI-TSUNG'S POEM

Lush blossoming lies among azure calyces
And gleams throughout the whole courtyard:
As if drunk, soaked by the falling dew,
As though molten, lit through rose-colored clouds.
He who paints in bright colors
*   cannot use his brush here—*
Creation alone leaves the masterpiece.
Dancing butterflies stray along fragrant paths,
And fluttering, chase the wind of evening.

Translated by Stephen Owen

The emperor Hui-tsung was a skilled calligrapher and a poet of great subtlety. His verse above plays on the traditional poetic identification of flowers with courtesans and of butterflies with young men of leisure. A languid "lush blossoming," a woman, attracts young men, or "dancing butterflies," on a twilit evening beyond the ability of a painter to recreate. The detail opposite, which is the character for "drunk," reveals the complex beauty of the emperor's brushwork.

The majestic peak in Fan K'uan's Traveling Among Streams and Mountains towers over two tiny travelers and their mules (at lower right), reflecting the isolation of the artist himself. Fan lived as a hermit, "daily observing the clouds, mist, [and] melancholic ways of wind and moon...," according to his biography in Hui-tsung's catalog.

OPPOSITE: BRUSHWORK DETAIL FROM HUI-TSUNG'S POEM

Around 1050, when the art of landscape painting was already in full flower, a little-known painter named Ch'ü Ting created the vast panorama at right, Summer Mountains. *The viewer is meant to experience this landscape both as a whole and as a series of vignettes. The eye travels through the scene beginning at the right, where fishermen are lowering the sails of their boats and flocks of geese fly over a village. To the left of the village a wayfarer on a donkey, followed by a servant, crosses a bridge, perhaps hoping to reach one of the pavilions in the mountains before nightfall. Around the travelers, an early evening mist rises from the forests and rolls up the mountains that recede into infinite space.* Ch'ü Ting achieved the enormous vistas of Summer Mountains *on a scroll that is but three feet wide, intended not for public display but for intimate viewing by one or two people. Among those who have held this scroll are Hui-tsung, whose seals are on the painting's border (not shown) and the Ch'ing emperor Ch'ien-lung, who wrote a twelve-line commentary in the upper right corner in 1748.*

古秀芸岑歲月
多鍾題孫重評
宣和印看異物
開生面渾是說
池窩墮牽棠好溜
夏山串帝翠雲發
嗜晴峽漸塌波
高樓百尺軒而
敲試一馮欄快
竟何
戊辰新正月
御題

Chinese artists were as adept at lively, realistic scenes as at monumental landscapes. In these three details from Chao Kan's tenth-century scroll A River Journey at First Snowfall, fishermen huddle for warmth on a raised platform (top), another lowers his net into the water (above), and boatmen in punts (opposite) bend to their poles as a cold wind ruffles the reeds and water.

V

THE FORBIDDEN CITY

OF THE MING

There is no greater pleasure," Genghis Khan once declared, "than to conquer one's enemies, to pursue them, to seize their property, to see their families in tears, to ride their horses and to ravish their women." All the male children of the nomadic Mongol tribes that Genghis united were trained for war from their earliest years. At the age of three they were strapped to the backs of horses until they could ride; at five they learned to use their fathers' bows and arrows; at fourteen they went into the army and stayed until they were killed in battle or reached the age of sixty and were allowed to retire. Every nonmilitary task was performed by slaves, by prisoners of war, or by women. As for the arts and crafts, for gourmandizing, and for literature, no warrior of Genghis would embarrass himself with such soft-handed conceits.

The fighting forces thus developed were the most powerful and the most ruthless the world had ever known. Attacking a town, the Mongols herded throngs of captured peasants in front

The emperor Yung-lo, third ruler in the Ming dynasty, built a new capital at Peking with a grand imperial residence—the Forbidden City.

of their ranks to take the brunt of the defenders' arrows. They slaughtered the inhabitants of any town that resisted them, as a warning to others and also to keep their rear free of guerrillas.

For all the grotesque savagery, the Mongols were highly disciplined and organized. The Mongol cavalry that swept across Asia and into Europe did not fight en masse, as the phrase "Mongol horde" implies; rather, Genghis Khan organized his vast army in units similar to the divisions, companies, and platoons of a modern force. In the field these units performed with precision, coordinating their movements by a signal system of flags, torches, and whistling arrows. Thus two columns, converging on an enemy, could stage a pincer maneuver with perfect timing.

With tactics like these the Mongols conquered vast territories from Korea to Poland and Hungary, from Moscow to Baghdad, and to the eastern shores of the Mediterranean. Genghis Khan and his successors ruled this empire by a system of strict laws that Genghis himself drew up. These encompassed all areas of human activity and were administered by Mongol chieftains and foreigners brought into conquered lands. The local inhabitants were employed only in minor positions; the routes of advancement through the civil service were closed to them.

In 1218, when he had conquered much of north China, Genghis Khan summoned a distinguished Khitan aristocrat to his court in Mongolia–Yeh-lü Ch'u-ts'ai, whom he hoped to enlist in the Mongol service. Genghis had already been advised by his counselors that the Chinese were of no use. "It would be better," his advisers said, "to kill them all and turn the land back to pasture so that we can feed our animals on it."

But Yeh-lü Ch'u-ts'ai disagreed. "Now that you have conquered everywhere under Heaven and all the riches of the four seas," he told the Khan, "you can have everything you want, but you have not yet organized it. You can set up taxation on land and merchants; you should make profits on wine, salt, iron and the produce of the mountains and marshes. In this way in a single year you will obtain 500,000 ounces of silver, 80,000 rolls

Genghis Khan, a ruthless military genius, began the conquest of China, crushed the middle eastern nation of Khwarizm, and sent an expeditionary force into Russia. His heirs created history's largest empire, stretching from Korea to Hungary.

of silk, and 400,000 sacks of grain. How can it be said that the Chinese people are of no use to you?"

Genghis was convinced by this argument and instead of devastating China, he colonized it. The Mongols were gradually so influenced by Chinese ideas and values that a new process of assimilation took place. Once again a foreign race and a foreign culture merged into the developing civilization of China. The Chinese view of history as "change within tradition" was once more confirmed. Under the benign influence of Yeh-lü Ch'u-ts'ai, now the official scribe-secretary and astrologer-astronomer, Genghis' successor, Ogadei, allowed the Chinese more and more influence over their own affairs; and eventually the civil service was once again opened to them. A generation later Genghis Khan's grandson Kublai Khan decided to move the Mongol capital from Karakorum, far north beyond the Great Wall, to the city of Chung-tu, which he renamed Ta-tu and which is now Peking. Here he built that immense walled city, which under his successors became one of the splendors of the East.

Even in Kublai Khan's own day, Ta-tu was a city of mysterious wonders to the outside world. Leading to it, through the measureless expanses of the Mongol empire, were post roads, begun by Genghis Khan and improved and extended by his successors. On these roads there were stables and inns at regular intervals; runners, horsemen, and, in the north, teams of dogs pulling sleds carried messages and goods. The runners, who covered their three-mile stages in not much more than a quarter of an hour, wore bells at their waists and carried flaming torches at night. Caravans of merchants and parties of travelers rode these post roads to the empire of the Great Khan. Patrolled by Mongol cavalry, the road system was so safe that one contemporary chronicler wrote with pride, "a maiden bearing a nugget of gold on her head could wander safely through the realm."

In 1260 Kublai declared that a new dynasty, eventually called the Yüan (the Original), had been created. Kublai Khan was a stern ruler who lived in great pomp. He was transported in state

Resplendent in an ermine cloak, Kublai Khan, a grandson of Genghis, rides out on a hunt. After completing the conquest of China in 1279, Kublai revived the devastated country; but later Mongol rulers were harsh and were resented by the Chinese.

from Ta-tu to his summer palace in a grand parade of elephants. The Great Khan sat in a magnificent litter, covered outside with lion skins and inside with cloth of gold. Whenever the brilliant cavalcade halted, servants would quickly erect hundreds of tents and the Khan's splendid marquee, which was lined with ermine and sable and supported by columns of sweetly scented wood.

Kublai Khan was no sybarite, however. He painstakingly organized several ambitious military campaigns, conquering Yünnan, invading Burma and burning its capital, and sending a punitive force to Java to avenge an insult on a Mongol ambassador. He sent a huge armada against Japan, but it was destroyed by the divine wind, the *kamikaze*, a name associated with the suicidal heroes of a much later conflict. But as well as being an avenging warlord, Kublai Khan was also a wise and understanding ruler. He allowed Christian missionaries to preach in his cities, and he encouraged an ever-increasing trade with the outside world. All manner of Chinese inventions went westward to Europe, such as gunpowder, printing, playing cards, and textiles. To China came new techniques in bronze, ceramics, glass, and enamel, as well as new kinds of food and wine.

But within fifteen years of the death of the great Kublai in 1294, the Mongol empire began to crumble. Corrupt administration and harsh taxation led to peasant revolts that the Mongol garrisons—no longer hardy, disciplined warriors of the steppes—were unable to suppress. And in one of these revolts there arose a revolutionary of peasant stock and remarkable pockmarked ugliness. In 1368, following the precedent of the peasant rebel who had founded the Han dynasty at the end of the third century B.C., this man founded the Ming dynasty.

This fourteenth-century peasant, Chu Yüan-chang, came from a poor family in Anhui province. The youngest of four sons, he alone had survived when a swarm of locusts devoured what few crops had remained in his family's fields after a drought. He entered a Buddhist monastery as a novice, but having no vocation for such a life, he wandered for three years as a beggar

One way the Chinese expressed their reverence for the past was in their passion for collecting antiques. The title of this fifteenth-century scroll, Enjoying Antiquities, *conveys the sensuous pleasure two gentlemen derive from handling ancient bronzes and ceramics in the tranquillity of a garden.*

until hunger drove him back to the monastery once more. Soon afterward a large force of rebels appeared in the district, and the nineteen-year-old Chu Yüan-chang ran off to join them. The rebel leader, impressed by the astonishingly ugly young man's evident force of character, accepted him and later gave him a young orphan girl for a wife. A few years later, a rebel commander himself, Chu captured Ta-tu, driving out the last Mongol emperor, who spent most of his days making clocks.

Historians of the Ming dynasty were to deify its founder, to present him as a divine savior, to surround his career with portents and legends. When his mother was pregnant with him, so they said, she had dreamed of a divine spirit who gave her a pill that glowed when placed in her palm. "She swallowed it and when she awoke, a fragrant essence lingered in her mouth. When she gave birth, a red glow filled the house. From this night on the glow appeared repeatedly...wherever her son slept...When he was grown to manhood, his presence was wonderfully heroic and superlatively strong."

He became the "Great Ancestor, the Heaven-Opening, the Way-Implementing, Dynasty-Founding, Pinnacle-Standing, Greatly Worthy, Most Holy, Benevolent, Cultivated, Righteous, Martial, Refined, Virtuous and Successful Exalted Emperor." Chu Yüan-chang, who took the reign name Hung-wu, was anxious to disown his humble origins. "I intend to rule like the T'ang and the Sung," he declared.

Certainly he reunited the empire as the T'ang and Sung had done and reconquered lost territories. He revived the moribund civil service examinations, and established a system of state schools: examinees had to sit for days in little separate cubicles, endeavoring to pass first the preliminary examinations in the prefectural capital, then the secondary examinations in the provincial capital, and finally the third examinations in the imperial capital, using the same books that had been set for study by Sung scholars, writing essays in the prescribed eight sections, commenting upon quotations from the classics. As in the past, successful candidates became part of a privileged elite, exempt from taxation and labor service.

Yet, often as Hung-wu spoke of rooting out Mongol institutions and replacing them with those of the T'ang and the Sung, he retained many Mongol practices, among them the rigid classification of families and occupations, which ensured, for instance, that a miner remained a miner and his son became a miner. Hung-wu also introduced new practices, such as corporal punishment for government officials found guilty of some offense. Previously such men had to commit suicide but were never publicly humiliated. Now they were flogged with such severity that several died, and officials took to congratulating each other when they returned home from the capital unscathed.

Hung-wu was, in fact, a far more absolute monarch than his Sung predecessors. So, also, were the emperors who followed him. Less paranoid than the founder, they encouraged contact with the outside world. A series of extraordinary maritime expeditions from 1405 to 1433 went into far distant uncharted seas, into the Indian Ocean and the Persian Gulf, south to Borneo, and perhaps even to Australia. (In 1879 a statuette of the Ming period was found inside a baobab tree near Darwin.) It is probable that Chinese sailors rounded the southern coast of Africa almost two centuries before European sailors crossed those seas from the west. Partly in pursuit of trade, partly in search of knowledge, these embassies sailed in larger, more imposing ships than any in Western waters.

Political opposition and high costs brought an end to the explorations about sixty years before the Portuguese navigator Vasco da Gama sailed around the Cape of Good Hope in 1497, opening Asia to European trade and colonization. During the early sixteenth century, the Portuguese rapidly established a string of trading bases all along the African and Asian coasts, reaching out even to China, where Portuguese merchants settled at Macao in 1555. As the Europeans reaped a fortune from carrying Chinese goods to the rest of Asia, the Ming emperors

The Sacred Way leading to Hung-wu's tomb is lined with stone elephants, camels, and other protective figures.

THE MING TOMBS

In crypts beneath earthen mounds, protected by carved stone figures (above) of animals, generals, and officials, the Ming emperors and empresses lie buried with their greatest treasures. The tomb of the first Ming emperor, Hung-wu, is outside his capital of Nanking. All but two of his successors are buried north of Peking in the Valley of the Thirteen Tombs. Here robbers broke into the crypt of the emperor Hsüan-te in 1937 and took a hoard of gold objects, including the plaque at right, one of the few pieces from the trove that has been traced. In 1956 archaeologists found twenty-six chests of treasure in the tomb of Wan-li, an extravagant ruler who spent eight million ounces of silver on the construction of his crypt and held a party inside when it was finished.

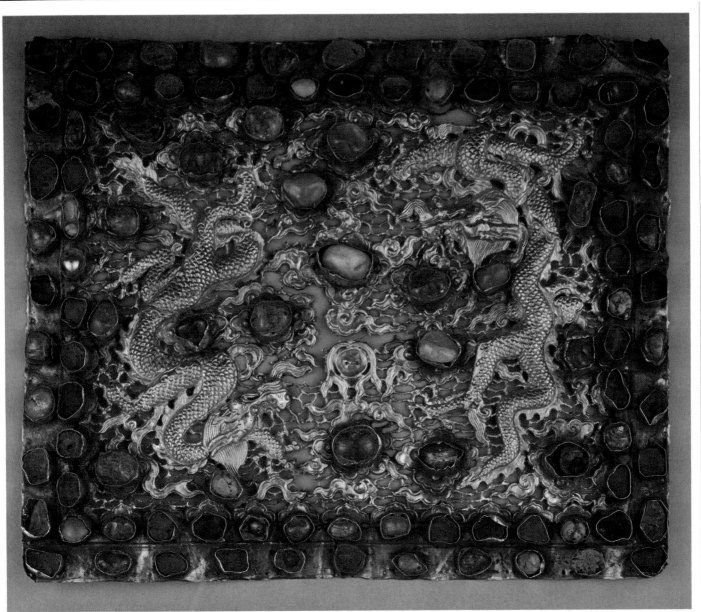

Two golden dragons writhe amid semiprecious stones on the plaque above, one of an identical pair designed to be sewn on the emperor's robe.

banned the construction of oceangoing ships, forbade their merchants from leaving China, and turned inward.

Many art forms flourished under the Ming. Craftsmen made rugs and carpets more beautiful than had ever been before. Architecture flourished–Ming architects built lovely bridges, temples, villas, shrines, and pagodas that can still be seen throughout China, as well as magnificent tombs outside Peking, where thirteen Ming emperors are buried, with an avenue lined by majestic stone elephants, camels, and mythical beasts. Painting also thrived during the years of Ming rule; the number of paintings–many of great vitality and originality–was enormous. But principally the Ming are now remembered for their ceramics. Most of these beautifully colored porcelain wares were made at Ching-te-chen, a town in Kiangsi near the hill known as Kao-ling, from which kaolin takes its name. Out of it came that fine white clay ideal for the making of porcelain. Ching-te-chen, rebuilt in 1369, was entirely given over to the ceramics industry, and remained its center until the middle of the nineteenth century.

Many of the loveliest pieces of Ming porcelain were destined for the former Mongol capital of Ta-tu, rebuilt by the emperor Yung-lo and renamed Peking, meaning Northern Capital. Following the traditional Sung pattern and adapting the plan of cities within a city, Peking was built by a million workmen over a period of at least ten years in the form of a grid. The Imperial City, surrounded by the walls and buildings of the outer city, itself enclosed the apartments and palaces of the court. This inner core, known as the Forbidden City, was surrounded by its own high wall and had gates in each of its four sides, the Gates of Eastern and Western Glory, the northern Gate of Spiritual Valor, and the southern Meridian Gate.

From a terrace over the Meridian Gate the emperor reviewed his imperial guard; and through this gate, using portals assigned according to rank, walked officials, military officers, and vassals on their way to state receptions. After these dignitaries had

A group of ministers (above), whose colored robes denote their official ranking (red, blue, and green, in descending order), gather beneath willow trees in a detail from a scroll painting of an imperial entourage leaving a palace.

passed, two files of elephants flanking the gate stepped together and locked their trunks to bar the way. On the other side of the Meridian Gate a winding canal, called the River of Golden Water, formed a decorative moat spanned by five bridges. Beyond the moat another gate led to an imposing courtyard, six hundred feet wide, calculated to overawe visitors as they approached the Hall of Supreme Harmony.

This building–today the oldest surviving timber structure in China–held the Dragon Throne, where the emperor presided on the most solemn occasions. In a subsidiary throne hall–the Hall of Protecting Harmony–missions from Korea, Japan, Tibet, Annam (Vietnam), Siam, and many other lands presented tribute to the Ming emperors, recognizing Chinese political and cultural supremacy over the whole Far East. Twice a year religious duties took the emperor outside the walls of the Forbidden and Imperial cities to the Temple of Heaven precinct in southern Peking. There at two temples, among the masterpieces of Chinese architecture, the emperor prayed and offered sacrifices.

The utter seclusion and luxury of life within the Forbidden City caused the later Ming emperors to lose interest in the affairs of state. With little gift or taste for government most of them left decisions to bickering courtiers and eunuchs. Emperor Wan-li never once had an audience with an official in his twenty-five-year reign, dealing with them entirely through eunuchs. Hung-wu had refused to tolerate more than a hundred eunuchs at his court, but Wan-li kept over 100,000 in the various Imperial Palaces–an ominous shadow government. The regular bureaucracy distrusted this unnatural influence over imperial policy and disliked the financial burdens the eunuchs imposed upon the state.

Of such abuses at court the ordinary millions of Chinese knew little. To them the emperor was a distant, almost mystical figure. It was their landlords who dominated their lives. A typical estate was that of Madame Kung, the aunt of a well-known official. At dawn her hundred serfs would report to her. Those she considered lazy she had flogged, while she prepared a goblet of wine for

One of the ablest administrators of the Ming period, Yang Jung (above) served five emperors in the fifteenth century. As a grand secretary, Yang Jung exerted a moderating influence amid the bickering and intrigue at court.

the diligent. "In this way," according to Fu I-ling, a modern-day historian, "everyone whom Madame employed proved himself capable; her lands supported cattle by the hundred, her streams bred fish and turtles by the cartload; and her gardeners tended fruit, melons, mustard and vegetables by the tens of acres."

Many estate owners won the loyalty of their serfs by going with them into the fields to supervise the backbreaking toil of ploughing and sowing, but many landowners treated their peasants with cruelty or contempt. And in some cases the peasants rose up and if not subjugated or claimed by some other landlord, they might join one of the rebel bands that sprang up all over China in the later years of the Ming. One of the most powerful rebel leaders was an army deserter named Li Tzu-ch'eng, another of those gifted and ambitious peasants who have emerged from the time of Lao-tzu to that of Mao Tse-tung to change the course of their country's history.

In 1643, with a huge force at his command, Li Tzu-ch'eng captured Sian and advanced upon Peking. Two thirds of the 150,000 troops that usually guarded the city had fled or deserted to join the rebels. The eunuch in command of the southern gate turned traitor and opened it to the insurgents. Li's men poured into the city as the last Ming emperor fled from his palace to a pavilion on Meishan Hill. Flames already enveloped the Forbidden City. In his blood he wrote a final message: "My virtue is small, and therefore I have incurred the anger of Heaven and rebels have captured my capital." Then he removed the girdle from his robe and hanged himself.

But Li Tzu-ch'eng's power was not to last. Out on the northern frontier, a Ming general had been defending the Great Wall against a barbarian invader–the Manchu. Li Tzu-ch'eng now called upon this general to join him. But the general decided that the Manchu were less fearsome than the peasant rebels of his own country. He allowed them to cross the wall, joined forces with them against Li Tzu-ch'eng, and thus helped establish a new foreign dynasty in China.

WHERE EARTH AND SKY MEET

The gates, halls, and palaces of the Forbidden City are protected from malevolent spirits by fearsome lions such as the one above, made of gilded bronze.

According to Chinese belief, the emperor stood at the center of the universe—figuratively the North Star, around whom the heavens revolve. In 1416 this concept was embodied in the design of Peking, which the emperor Yung-lo ordered his architects to build "in Harmony with the Universe." In the center of the humming, turbulent capital they built a walled enclosure for official buildings and parks called the Imperial City. At its center was the Forbidden City, a 250-acre complex—protected by walls and a moat—of palaces, pavilions, vast courtyards, and gardens where the emperor dwelled in serene isolation. His sanctum is replete with emblems of his status as the Son of Heaven: the yellow-tiled roofs take their color, reserved for the emperor, from the sun; the walls are reddish-purple, a color associated with the North Star; and the main entrance (right) is the Meridian Gate—the sun at its zenith. Through this gate the emperor passed on his way to the Temple of Heaven, in the southern section of Peking, to speak to the supreme deity, the Great Spirit Who Resides in Heaven.

Within the Forbidden City are seventy-five buildings, including three great throne halls named the Halls of Supreme, Central, and Protecting Harmony, after Confucian concepts. The northern part of the complex is devoted to magnificent gardens of artificial grottoes, winding paths, congeries of exotically shaped rocks brought down from mountains and up from lake bottoms, arches of cloven cypress trees and even a miniature mountain. This private landscape is the culmination of a private world, the symbolic center of the city, the nation, and the universe where all forces were believed to be in harmony and, according to an ancient text, "where the four seasons merge, where wind and rain are gathered in . . . and earth and sky meet."

The serpentine walls of the River of Golden Water (right) wind through the courtyard behind the Meridian Gate in the Forbidden City.

Fanciful earthenware creatures, such as these (above) in the Forbidden City, line the roofs of nearly every important Chinese building. The man seated on a hen at left is Prince Min, a despotic ruler of the third century B.C. who was hanged from an eave for his cruelty. The Chinese made it a

custom to display an effigy of Min, as a warning to other tyrants, on rooftops along with a series of guardian animals that prevent the spirit of the hated prince from escaping. The large figure on the right is a ch'ih-wen—a dragon that is fond of water and protects buildings from fire.

The emperor used the Dragon Throne (left) in the Hall of Supreme Harmony on the most solemn state occasions, such as his birthday, the New Year, and the nomination of generals before a campaign. On those days the smoke of incense rose from the urns on the right, in nearby galleries bells of gold and jade sounded as the emperor ascended the six-foot-high platform to the throne. Flanking the throne are two cloisonné cranes symbolizing long life. Like the buildings in the Forbidden City, the throne faces south, the direction from which benevolent spirits come.

Celestial blue tiles (above) in the Temple of Heaven complex are stamped with dragons flying through clouds—a symbol of heaven.

Every spring the emperor prayed for a good harvest in the Temple of Heaven (left). For its perfect proportions and lavish but subtle use of colors the building has been called "the most beautiful single creation in all China."

OVERLEAF: *A network of brackets supports the dome of the Imperial Heavenly Vault, near the Temple of Heaven. Structurally the brackets make central pillars unnecessary and, in their intricate clusters, provide a decorative embellishment.*

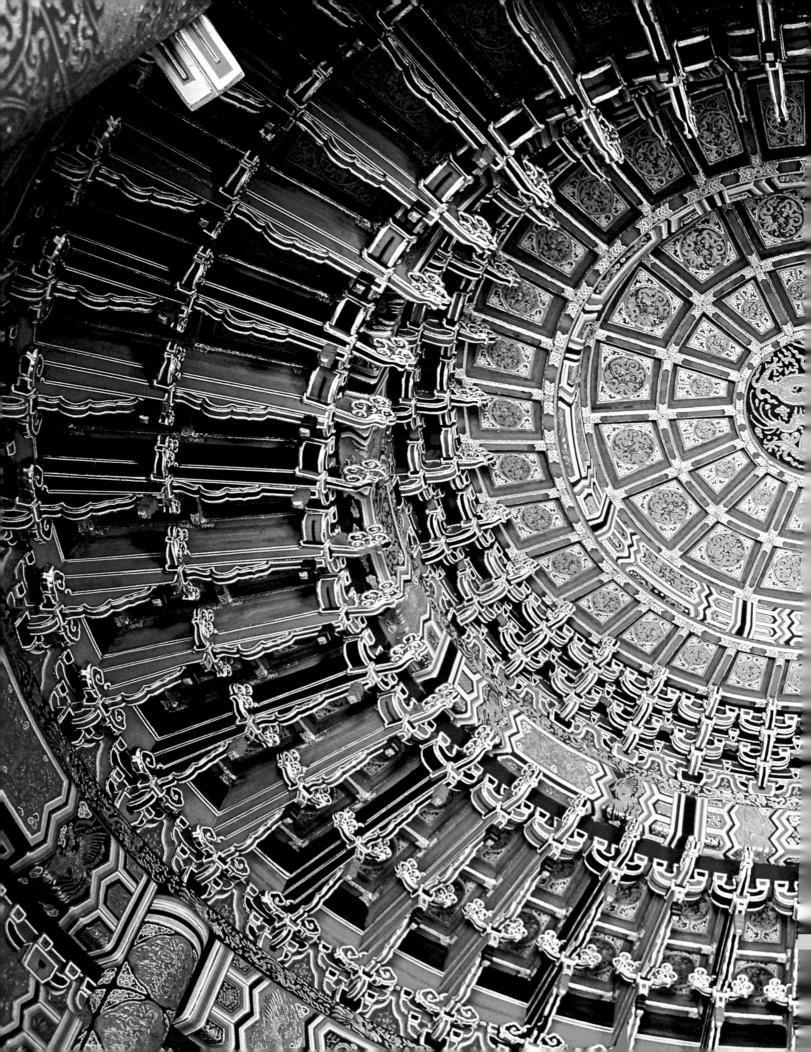

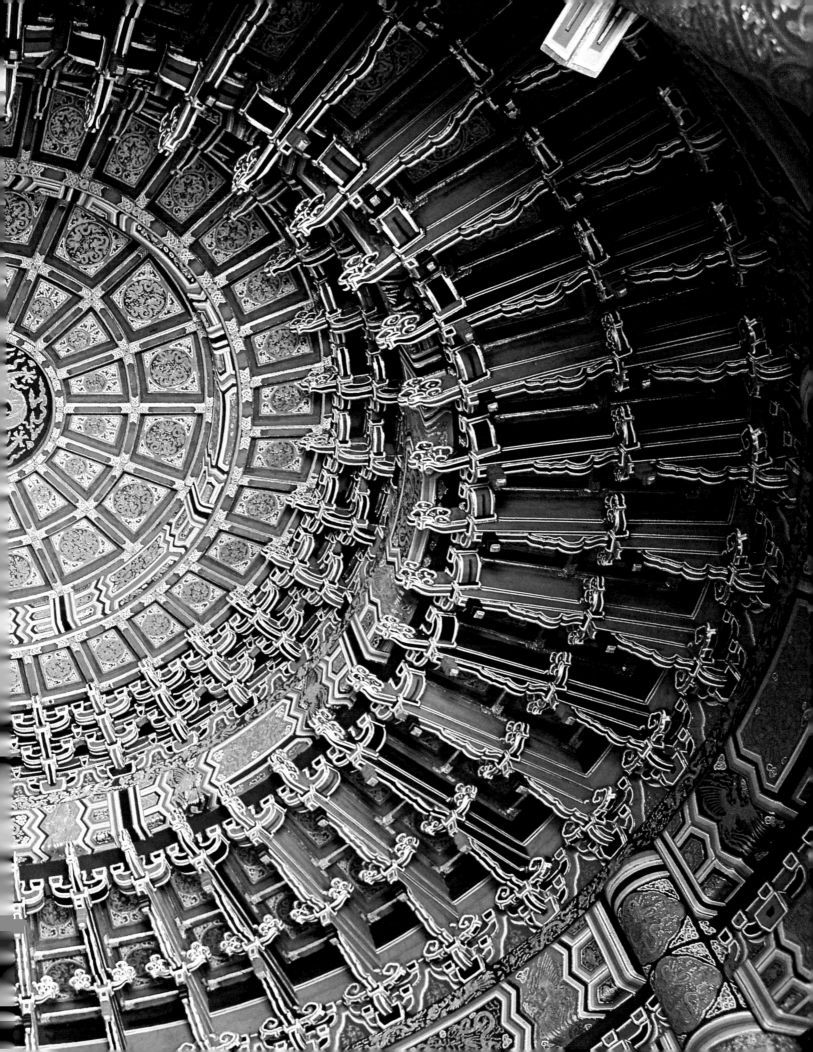

VI

EMPEROR CH'IEN-LUNG

OF THE CH'ING DYNASTY

Sweeping down from Tartary the Manchu invaders entered Peking in June 1644 and proclaimed the new Ch'ing dynasty. Like other conquerors before them, they were prepared to adopt traditional Chinese methods and philosophies including Confucianism in order to maintain their rule. But they were determined to subjugate the Chinese people and to present themselves as the master race. They changed the official dress of the country to the Tartar dress with its side fastenings and high stiff collar; they obliged the men of China to shave their heads and wear pigtails; they forced them to recognize that the Tartar was a member of a privileged elite. Even though a Chinese official might be of the same rank as his Manchu counterpart and entitled to wear the same color button in his mandarin's hat, the social barrier between the two was not to be bridged.

In the long reign of the renowned Manchu emperor K'ang-hsi, from 1662 to 1722, began an expansion of empire and an increase in prosperity that were to mark the dynasty's greatest ep-

Emperor Ch'ien-lung, in his dragon robe opposite, reigned over 300 million Chinese subjects during the last half of the eighteenth century.

Silkworm harvesters gather the finest mulberry leaves for the voracious and highly valued insects. This scene and the one opposite are from a series of Ch'ing dynasty engravings.

och. K'ang-hsi and his immediate successors took Turkestan and Ili, reduced the Burmese and Nepalese to suzerainty, drove the Gurkhas out of Tibet, and even defeated the Russians near the river Amur in Siberia. The empire grew ever larger, stretching from the Siberian forests beside the Amur in the north to the tropical mountains of the south. This vast empire was so rich and the imperial exchequer so replete that several times tax payments were canceled. The population increased dramatically; there were about 150 million people in China in 1700, some 275 million in 1779, and well over 300 million in 1794.

By this last date the imperial throne was occupied by K'ang-hsi's grandson Ch'ien-lung, the classic model of the cultivated emperor. He was a man of remarkable gifts and intellect, a scholar and a poet as well as an ambitious and merciless warrior. He was born in 1711, and even as a child, his extraordinary talents had been so unmistakable that K'ang-hsi decided this precocious boy should one day have the throne. Accordingly, the child was given a rigorous and thorough education. He was set to work at his lessons at five o'clock in the morning and not permitted to abandon them until the sun went down, except to be trained as an expert horseman and archer. At the age of twenty-four he was proclaimed emperor. He had by then fulfilled his early promise and become a slender, agile young man nearly six feet tall, lively, alert, and as regular in his habits then as he was to remain for the sixty years of his reign.

He rose every morning before dawn. After his bath—and surrounded by guards, standards, banners, umbrellas, and musicians—he was carried on a high palanquin to his private pagoda to worship Buddha. He then began his daily study of official papers, breaking off for a quick and frugal breakfast at seven o'clock. After this he would go for a walk in the palace garden, accompanied by several of his women and eunuchs. His favorite companions in his early days were his first wife, Empress Hsiao-hsien, whom he had married when he was sixteen; his second wife, Ula Nara, who was to retire to a monastery in 1765; and his lovely concubine Hsiang-fei, the widow of a prince from central Asia, who had been taken prisoner in one of his wars of conquest. He was said to love this woman above all others, but his mother distrusted her and ordered her to commit suicide during one of the emperor's periodical absences from court. He had at least a hundred other concubines to whom he could turn for consolation, as well as eight queens who all together bore him seventeen sons and ten daughters.

After his walk Ch'ien-lung conferred with his grand counselors and secretaries, then at three o'clock he had lunch. Like breakfast it was a solitary meal, and he ate little, sampling but a few of the many dishes that were offered to him, and never drinking alcohol at this or any other meal. He might spend the afternoon in a visit to the theater or in writing prose or poetry, talking to scholars, reading, painting, or practicing calligraphy. He rarely went to bed later than seven o'clock, having had the sparsest of evening meals. A eunuch remained on duty throughout the night to fetch any of the queens or concubines the emperor might feel disposed to call for. Sometimes he would wake in the night with a sudden inspiration, take up his brush and ink, and begin writing again. At least forty thousand poems have been attributed to him.

Literature was by no means the only art Ch'ien-lung patronized. He encouraged calligraphers, painters, and architects as well as workers in jade, ivory, porcelain, and lacquer. He spent immense sums on the palaces at Peking and Mukden, on the summer palace of Yüan-ming Yüan at Ju-i kuan, and on the beautiful grounds of another summer palace at Jehol, beyond the Great Wall. There, in the Paradise of Countless Trees, groups of willows drooped their branches by the lotus-covered lake and shaded the rock pools, where gleaming fish darted in the clear water, and walnut trees and corianders, pears and apricots grew everywhere on the grass slopes. He built garden houses with gilt doors and roofs of porcelain tiles, ornate gateways and clock towers, temples and pavilions, pagodas and painted bridges. Nor did

A family of silkworm cultivators congregate in a pavilion to give thanks to ancestor spirits for a successful season. Skeins of silk threads, hanging from a bamboo pole, adorn the altar.

he despise the arts of the West, as so many of his less enlightened mandarins did. He commissioned Jesuit missionaries to design buildings for him in a kind of Italianate style, and admired the paintings of European artists.

Yet Ch'ien-lung had little interest in Western sciences and Western thought. Indeed, he had no very sure idea where Europe was. Most of his officials had less. They knew, of course, as Chinese officials had always known, that China was the center of the world. Beyond the empire's frontiers lay the lands of the barbarians. They lived by trade, and the less the Celestial Empire had to do with these "foreign devils" the better. It was a crime for a Chinese to teach his language to a foreigner, and the export of any Chinese books was forbidden. Foreigners, apart from a few scattered missionaries and Jesuit architects, were not allowed inside China.

So, virtually the only contact between the Chinese and the countries of the West was between Chinese merchants and those few European and American traders who were permitted to carry on business in the far south of the empire, on the outskirts of the port of Canton, and on the nearby offshore island of Macao. For these foreign merchants—who had to transact all their business through a group of Chinese merchants known as the Cohong—the conditions of trade were most unsatisfactory. The Chinese exported tea, silk, rhubarb, porcelain and lacquer ware, and cotton fabric from Nanking known in Europe as nankeen, all of which had to be paid for in silver. It was an axiom of government that the Chinese people had no need of the inferior merchandise foreigners had to offer.

In hope of alleviating these difficulties, the merchants at Canton asked the British government to plead on their behalf at the imperial court at Peking. Accordingly, in September 1793 a delegation from London, headed by a gifted diplomatist, Lord Macartney, arrived in Peking with a large variety of precious gifts in padded boxes, a number of ingenious mechanisms demonstrating the inventive skills of the English race, a complimentary letter

With spears, bows and arrows, and tridents, a royal hunting party kills game in this anonymous painting made about 1700. After the hunt, the courtiers in all their finery retired to large tents for festive picnicking and dancing.

from the king of England, and portraits of the king and queen by Sir Joshua Reynolds. The bearer of these gifts was conducted to a huge pavilion in the Imperial Park at Jehol, where he was to be presented to the emperor. Ch'ien-lung's arrival was heralded by the sound of musical instruments, voices proclaiming his virtues and power, and the swish of silk robes of the attendant mandarins as they prostrated themselves on the ground at his feet. When the Son of Heaven had ascended the steps to his throne, Lord Macartney knelt before him and offered him the king of England's letter in a gold box encrusted with diamonds. The emperor accepted the letter and handed it to his chief minister who placed it, unread, upon a cushion.

During the "sumptuous banquet" that followed, Macartney was deeply impressed with the order and regularity with which the delicious food was served, and the "calm dignity and sober pomp of Asiatic greatness" with which "every function of the ceremony was performed": the "silence and solemnity resembled the celebration of a religious mystery." He was impressed, too, by the gracious condescension of the emperor who sent his party several dishes from his own table, together with goblets of warm rice wine, and then summoned the ambassador to him. He offered him a cup of wine with his own hands, and addressed several polite remarks to him, inquiring how old the king of England was and expressing the hope that he would live to the great age that the emperor himself had attained. Macartney thought the eighty-three-year-old man "a very fine gentleman."

Lord Macartney's hopes were raised still higher when he was later granted the unusual favor of a conducted tour of the Imperial Park at Jehol. Further compliments were bestowed upon Macartney and his suite when they were invited to the emperor's birthday celebrations. Yet whenever Macartney tried to discuss the purpose of his mission, he met evasions or pretended incomprehension. And when the emperor returned from Jehol to his summer palace at Yüan-ming Yüan, the foreigners were given strong hints that it was time for them to go home. They were

TEXT CONTINUED ON PAGE 152

SILKEN
DRAGONS

Though the Chinese aristocracy had always reveled in elaborate dress and official vestments, the dragon robes and informal tunics of the Ch'ing brought an opulence and theatricality never before seen in court costumes. Designers, weavers, and seamstresses devoted their lives to the royal robes, working with the finest textiles, pearls, coral beads, and threads of gold and silver. Ch'ing robes, three of which are here and on the following four pages, represent the pinnacle of silk weaving and embroidery in China.

Amply cut to fit the large Manchu frame—and often lined with fine furs—the robes are glamorous, but the glamor is tempered by the complex meanings of the designs. With heaven and earth embroidered throughout, the robes are symbolic of the natural world and the entire universe, all under the dominion of the emperor—who appears as a dragon. The human body, representing the spiritual axis of the garments, completes the symbolism.

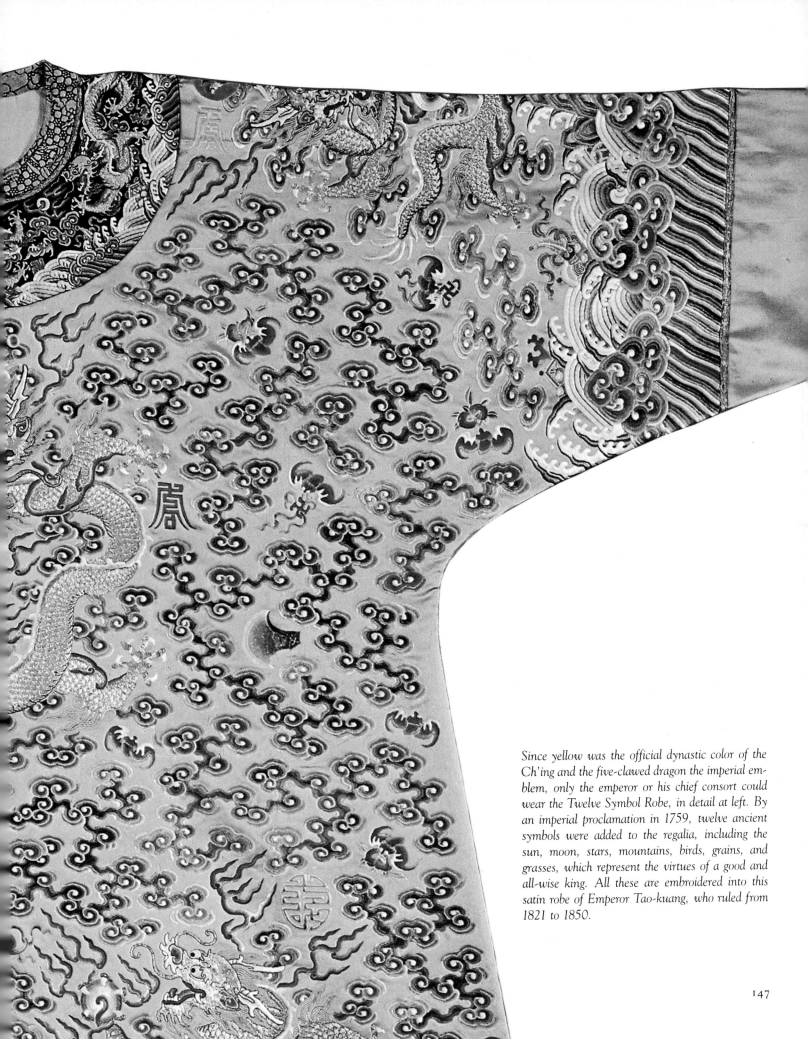

Since yellow was the official dynastic color of the Ch'ing and the five-clawed dragon the imperial emblem, only the emperor or his chief consort could wear the Twelve Symbol Robe, in detail at left. By an imperial proclamation in 1759, twelve ancient symbols were added to the regalia, including the sun, moon, stars, mountains, birds, grains, and grasses, which represent the virtues of a good and all-wise king. All these are embroidered into this satin robe of Emperor Tao-kuang, who ruled from 1821 to 1850.

The world is beautiful and full of life in these two details from the imperial dragon robe below. At left, a bat—an emblem of happiness—hovers above a sea of gold and silver threads, as the five-clawed dragon, opposite, made of coral beads and pearls, grasps at red flames of wisdom. The patterned circle near the dragon's right hind claw is a shou, an emblem of longevity.

This silk-embroidered satin dragon robe belonged to the Ch'ing emperor T'ung-chih, who ruled from 1862 to 1873.

Narcissus and other flowers—including cherry blossoms entwined in stylized vases—are embroidered in multicolored silk and gilt thread across the deep blue woolen broadcloth of this informal tunic. The woman who wore it, a contemporary of the empress dowager Tz'u-hsi in the late nineteenth century, is the figure in the ivory satin border, out for a garden stroll.

In a detail from a seventeenth-century painting on silk, a couple—probably a Ch'ing official and his concubine—embrace in an elegant garden pavilion.

TEXT CONTINUED FROM PAGE 145

requested to deliver a letter to the king of England that, so Macartney later discovered, had been written before their arrival. This letter informed the king that "the local products" which had been presented to him as "tribute articles" had been received, but that such ingenious articles had never been valued in China, which had not "the slightest need" of England's manufactures. The letter ended, "You, O King, should simply act in conformity with our wishes by strengthening your loyalty and swearing perpetual obedience."

Despite this rebuff, the British government decided to send another embassy to China in 1816. In 1799, Ch'ien-lung had died; the new emperor was Chia-ch'ing, the fifth son of Ch'ien-lung by one of his concubines. He was a clever and hardworking man, but he was also obstinate, deceitful, cold, and avaricious. On coming to the throne he had had his father's immensely rich chief minister arrested and tortured.

Chia-ch'ing then appropriated the minister's enormous collection of treasures that, guarded by four hundred watchmen, included no less than nine thousand solid gold scepters and fifty-six huge pearl necklaces as well as vast quantities of gold and enamel watches, lacquer furniture inlaid with precious stones, and snuff bottles of carnelian and amber, jade and topaz. Chia-ch'ing went through the inventory with that obsessional concern for detail with which he supervised the most trivial aspects of court ceremonial, such ceremonial being a matter of far deeper concern to him than the ruling of his empire, as his dealings with the new embassy from England were to demonstrate. He simply sent the new ambassador home.

Having failed to remove by diplomacy the intolerable restrictions imposed upon their trade with China, the foreign merchants at Canton now advocated force. The result of this pressure was the fearful Opium War, so called because opium, smuggled into China from the East India Company's estates in Bengal, was now a spectacularly profitable commodity to both foreign and Chinese merchants. The Cantonese officials took immense bribes to turn a blind eye to the traffic, and by 1835 the number of addicts in China had increased to more than two million. The Treaty of Nanking, which brought the first Opium War to an end in 1842, was the beginning of a series of humiliations imposed upon China by force and eventually culminating in the looting and burning of the palace of Yüan-ming Yüan by French and British troops.

Sackfuls and cartloads of treasures, many of them made under the patronage and encouragement of Ch'ien-lung, were carried away by the soldiers. Silver clocks and rosewood tables, red-lacquered chests—in whose drawers, cracked open with bayonets, were found jewels of incalculable value—porcelain vases, jade ornaments, temple idols, enamel screens, crystal chandeliers, gilt looking glasses, embroidered silk robes and fans, mechanical toys, crackleware bowls, pictures, and books were all tipped into wagons, piled in broken fragments on the garden paths or smashed with rifle butts, and shot to pieces on the walls. Among the plunder were scores of "very pretty little dogs" of a breed for which it was a capital offense for anyone outside the imperial family to keep. One of them, a Pekingese Lion Dog appropriately named Looty, was presented to Queen Victoria.

The British empire was now approaching the days of its most impressive splendor; but the great days of the Chinese empire, despite the arrogance of its leading officials, were gone forever. The spiteful, fussy Chia-ch'ing was not the emperor to repair the damage; nor was his successor, the moody, vacillating Tao-kuang; nor Tao-kuang's dissipated son. Most ill suited of all to the Dragon Throne was the unhappy, lonely Kuang-hsü, who in abject submission to his aunt, the remarkable Empress Dowager Tz'u-hsi, unwillingly presided over the empire in its sad and final decline. Misgovernment was attended in many areas by devastating floods followed by drought, then by famine. Rebels were gathering in increasing numbers; secret societies were springing up like mushrooms, as the population of the country—which it is believed had risen to about 350 million by the middle of the

Hsiang-fei, Ch'ien-lung's favorite, waits for her imperial master. This detail is from a painting by an artist dubbed Lang Shih-ning, an Italian Jesuit who went to China as a missionary and became the emperor's court painter.

Tz'u-hsi, a former concubine who rose to rule the empire for its last half century, arranges her elaborate hairdo in the photograph above. By the time she died in 1908, China's imperial system had crumbled. Anarchy and revolution were at hand.

nineteenth century—was growing far faster than the cultivated areas of the country. An uprising of pseudo-Christian Taiping rebels, who claimed to have received "a Divine Commission to exterminate the Manchu," laid waste to vast areas of the country, and killed twenty million people before it was finally suppressed. The later rebellion of the Boxers—so called because they practiced a form of Taoist shadowboxing that they fancied made them impervious to their enemies' weapons—was antiforeign rather than anti-Manchu, and was accordingly supported by the wily empress dowager. But when the Boxers laid siege to the foreign legations in Peking, an international force landed in China and immediately crushed them.

This was in 1900. A few years later a young leader of the revolutionary United League wrote that despite the support the Boxers had briefly found, the Chinese had "come to realize that their country's woes stemmed from the Court and the Mandarins much more than the Europeans... Above all we are anti-Manchu, because this usurping dynasty has brought about our national decline."

The speaker was Sun Yat-sen, a peasant from the province of Kwangtung, who had been converted to Christianity and qualified as a doctor after leaving his mission school. In October 1911 the truly national revolution for which he had been working broke out at last: in one province after another the Manchu officials were overthrown. On January 1, 1912, Sun Yat-sen came to power. Once again a peasant had led forces that overthrew an imperial dynasty. But there were to be no more emperors. The new leader of China was photographed bareheaded in a European frock coat. He had been elected provisional president of the Chinese Republic. The uniquely Chinese character and continuity of Chinese civilization were to be preserved through the years of upheaval to come: change was to take place within an enduring framework of tradition. But the treasures of the Chinese emperors, which the centuries of imperial history had brought into being, were treasures of the past.

AN EMPEROR'S WHIMS

Pekingese pug dogs delighted eighteenth-century Emperor
Ch'ien-lung, who paraded his favorite pup in this brass cage.
Silk curtains once draped the tiny palace-on-wheels.

Emperor Ch'ien-lung presided over a secure and prosperous Manchu state (1736–1795) and was free to indulge his passions for reading, writing, poetry, calligraphy, and, especially, collecting art. One of the great patrons of all time, the emperor provided studios and stipends for masterworkers of enamel, glass, bronze, lacquer, gold, ivory, and jade. Insatiable, he dispatched his ministers to comb the provinces for the best of everything. When new treasures arrived–fine jewelry, porcelain bowls, enamel vases, lacquer boxes, intricate ivory carvings, silk brocades–the emperor proudly displayed some in his palaces and gave others away as extravagant gifts of state.

Ch'ien-lung favored enamel artists who cast vessels in elaborate animal shapes, and he preferred heavy gilding, bright greens, pinks, and yellows, and the flower and bird motifs of Chinese paintings. He insisted on an abundance of detail–in lacquer ware, for instance, he wanted every inch carved into decorative relief and inlaid with stones or precious metals. With the encouragement of Ch'ien-lung, tiny secret-compartment boxes became a famous Chinese art form. Ch'ien-lung particularly loved jade, in all its colors, and made sure he had it all: he simply decreed that hoarding or exporting the stone was a capital crime.

As the Han had appreciated sculptural rocks a thousand years earlier, Ch'ing royalty found beauty in gnarled birch. The root (right), a stand for a calligraphy brush, is also a piece of court flattery: it is carved to resemble a fungus, which, according to Chinese legend, grows during the reign of a virtuous monarch.

With feathers of red, indigo-blue, green, and yellow, this enamel wine container is a stylized but naturalistically colored representation of a duck. Ch'ien-lung had no interest in subtle colorings, and enamel artists heeded imperial preferences. After firing the glassy enamel pastes on the duck vessel, its creator probably spent months polishing and gilding his masterpiece.

Ch'ing customs dictated that the emperor travel with his throne, lest he hold court in an improper setting. Ch'ien-lung adhered to protocol and sent his lacquered and gilded throne–a detail from the back of it is below–ahead of him when he traveled from the Forbidden City.

Lacquer, the distilled resin of a common Chinese tree, had been used in ancient dynasties to finish crossbows, but under Ch'ien-lung, the art was brought to technical perfection. After carving wood into intricate shapes, craftsmen patiently applied coat after coat of clear lacquer (some used as many as three hundred thin layers of the resin), smoothing the surfaces with charcoal dust. To decorate their finest wares, lacquerers applied pigmented sap and inlaid gold, silver, and mother-of-pearl.

This seven-foot jade mountain (above and detail opposite) commemorates a superhero of Chinese mythology, Yü the Great, a legendary emperor who saved the empire from a terrible flood about 2000 B.C. According to the legend, Yü toiled unceasingly for nine years to harness the deluge, which was as catastrophic as the Biblical flood. In the detail, workmen are erecting dams to divert the waters. Later generations of Chinese so feared floods that they appeased the river god each year by drowning a young bride. The monumental sculpture—it weighs over ten thousand pounds—was created by several master jadesmiths in the fifty-third year of Ch'ien-lung's reign.

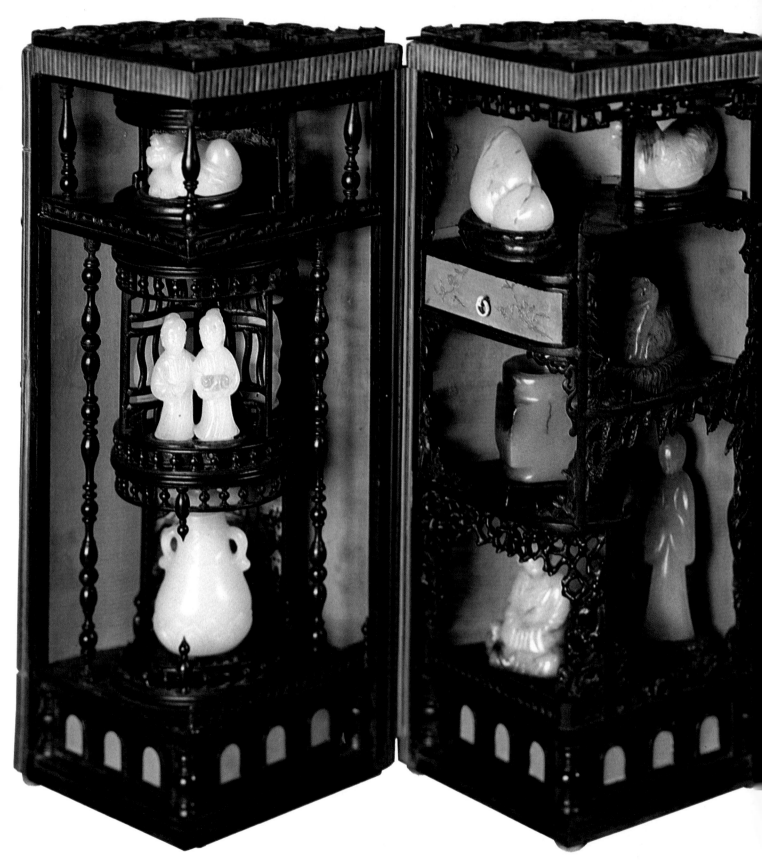

Less than ten inches high, Ch'ien-lung's treasure box, or to-pao-ko, holds figurines of jade. The drawers and doors in each quadrant open and close, and all eight of the windowed baseboards conceal secret compartments, which held miniature landscape scrolls. The box itself shuts up into a perfect cylinder.

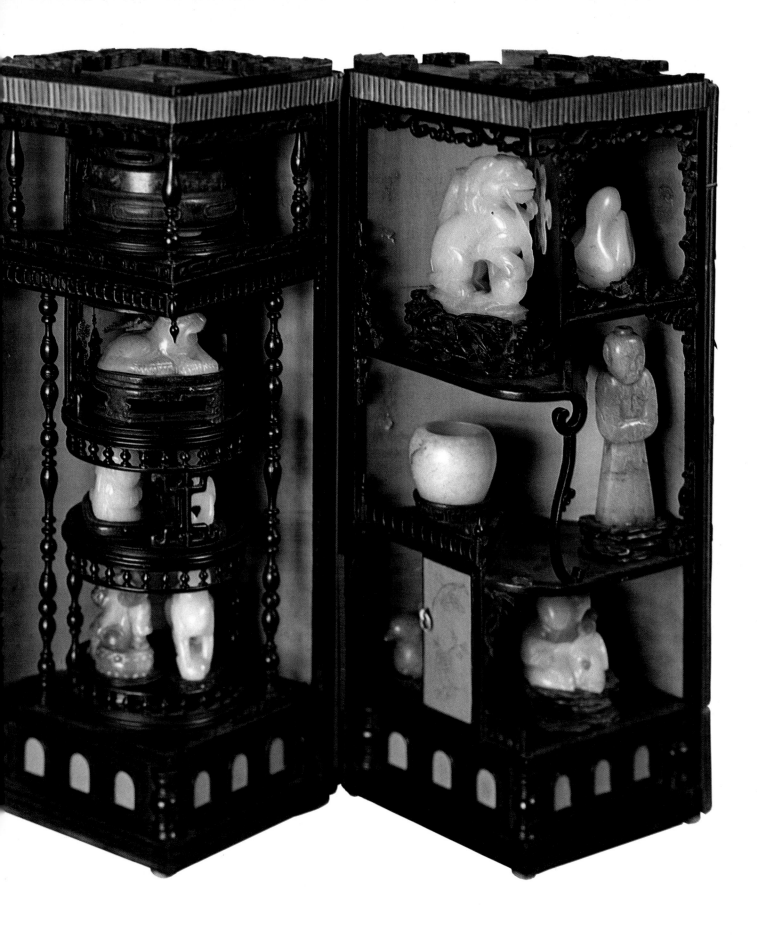

Nestled inside its cock-shaped lacquer case, the ivory dragon boat, above, is replete with multileveled cabins, railings, and

pennants. This whimsical treasure embodies two Chinese emblems: the beneficent dragon and the courageous rooster.

OVERLEAF: *Two impish servants carry a four-foot-long icebox. The bronze fixture is covered with enamel lotus blossoms, symbols of the hot season. Ch'ien-lung had coolers like this one filled with ice (harvested from northern lakes) to cool his summer palace near Peking. A golden lion surmounts the perforated lid.*

CHINA: A CHRONOLOGY

DYNASTY	PEOPLE AND EVENTS		CULTURE	
SHANG DYNASTY 16th c.–11th c. B.C.			1500 c. 1300	Bronze casting developed Oracle bones: earliest evidence of written Chinese
CHOU DYNASTY 11th c.–222 B.C.	11th c. 403–222 247	King Wu, founder Warring States period Tiger of Ch'in (later Shih Huang-ti) becomes king of Ch'in	6th c. c. 551–479 c. 470 c. 372–289 c. 300	Lao-tzu preaches Taoism Confucius lives and teaches *Analects* compiled by Confucius' followers Mencius continues spread of Confucianism First evidence of copper coins
CH'IN DYNASTY 221–207 B.C.	221–210 210 208	Ch'in Shih Huang-ti is emperor of united China Chao Kao controls government Li Ssu, prominent statesman, dies	221 c. 214 213 211	Legalism becomes state philosophy Great Wall completed Proscription and burning of books Shih Huang-ti's Spirit City completed, with thousands of clay and bronze figures
HAN DYNASTY Earlier Han 206 B.C.–A.D. 8	r. 206–195 r. 188–180 r. 141–87 c. 115 r. 33–8	Emperor Kao-tsu (Liu Pang) Empress Lü Emperor Wu-ti Expansion into central Asia Emperor Ch'eng-ti	c. 124 c. 113 c. 100	State examinations introduced Liu Sheng and Tou Wan buried in suits of jade Chinese begin trade with outside world

B.C.

A.D.

Later Han A.D. 25–220	r. 8–23 r. 25–57 184	Hsin dynasty, Emperor Wang Mang Emperor Liu Hsiu restores Han dynasty Yellow Turban Rebellion	c. 140	Silk Road opens

DYNASTY	PEOPLE AND EVENTS	CULTURE

SUI DYNASTY
A.D. 590–618

r. 590–604	Emperor Wen-ti (Yang Chien)
r. 605–618	Emperor Yang-ti
605–610	Grand Canal constructed between Yellow and Yangtze rivers

c. 590	Buddhist cave temple created at Lung-men
c. 600	Wood-block printing invented

T'ANG DYNASTY
A.D. 618–907

r. 626–649	Emperor T'ai-tsung Renewed expansion into central Asia
r. 649–683	Emperor Kao-tsung
r. 690–705	Empress Wu
r. 712–755	Emperor Ming-huang
755	An Lu-shan Rebellion
r. 849	Emperor Hsüan-tsung

c. 640	Ch'ang-an becomes cultural center
645	Hsüan-tsang brings Sanskrit scriptures from India
7th c.	Spread of Buddhism continues
c. 700	Glazed pottery figures as tomb treasures
7th–8th c.	Gold and silver smithing begins
c. 720	Li Po, Tu Fu, and Wang Wei leading poets
9th c.	Gunpowder invented for fireworks

SUNG AND YÜAN DYNASTIES

Northern Sung
A.D. 960–1126

Southern Sung
A.D. 1127–1279

Yüan
A.D. 1260–1368

r. 960–976	Emperor T'ai-tsu (General Chao K'uang-yin)
c. 1040	Gunpowder used in battle
r. 1068–1086	Emperor Shen-tsung
1086	Wang An-Shih, chief minister, dies
r. 1101–1125	Emperor Hui-tsung
1126	Nüchen Tartars capture Kaifeng and exile Hui-tsung
1127	Nüchen control north China Southern Sung dynasty established
r. 1127–1162	Emperor Kao-tsung
1135	Hangchow established as Southern Sung capital
1205	Genghis Khan begins invasion of China
r. 1260–1294	Kublai Khan rules as the Great Khan
1274	Attempted Mongol invasion of Japan
1279	Last Sung prince dies

10th–13th c.	Height of landscape painting
c. 1045	Invention of movable type
11th c.	Publishing centers flourish

MING DYNASTY
A.D. 1368–1644

r. 1368–1398	Emperor Hung-wu (Chu Yüan-chang)
r. 1403–1424	Emperor Yung-lo
1405–1433	Vast naval expeditions to Indian Ocean
r. 1426–1435	Emperor Hsüan-te
r. 1573–1620	Emperor Wan-li

14th–17th c.	Ming tombs built at Peking and Nanking
c. 1410–1424	Forbidden City constructed

CH'ING DYNASTY
A.D. 1644–1912

1644	Manchu invaders enter Peking; proclaim Ch'ing dynasty
r. 1662–1722	Emperor K'ang-hsi
r. 1736–1795	Emperor Ch'ien-lung
1793	Lord Macartney's embassy to China
r. 1796–1820	Emperor Chia-ch'ing
r. 1821–1850	Emperor Tao-kuang
1840–1842	Opium War
1842	Treaty of Nanking
1850	Taiping Rebellion breaks out
r. 1862–1873	Emperor T'ung-chih
r. 1875–1908	Emperor Kuang-hsü
1900–1901	Boxer Rebellion
1908	Empress Dowager Tz'u-hsi dies
1911	Republican Revolution breaks out
January 1, 1912	Sun Yat-sen elected provisional president of the Chinese Republic

17th c.	Jesuits settle in China under imperial patronage
1759	Imperial Twelve Symbol Robe created
18th c.	Dramatic population increase, from 150 million in 1700 to over 300 million in 1794

ACKNOWLEDGMENTS & CREDITS

Sources for the pictures in this book are shown below.
Abbreviations:
BM—British Museum, London
FGA—Smithsonian Institution, Freer Gallery of Art, Washington, D.C.
MFA—Museum of Fine Arts, Boston
MMA—Metropolitan Museum of Art, N.Y.
NPM—National Palace Museum, Taipei, Taiwan
ROM—Royal Ontario Museum, Toronto, Canada

We would like to thank the following for their assistance: Elaine Blanc, Skira Editions, S.A.; Wang Chi-wu, NPM; Levita Emery and Tom Haden, FGA; Ingrid de Kalbermatten, Office du Livre, Switzerland; Dr. Alfreda Murck and Suzanne Valenstein, Far Eastern Department, MMA; Elizabeth Routh, ROM; Ran Xiencui, *China Reconstructs*, Peking; Yu Zhichen, New China Pictures Company, Peking.

All maps by H. Shaw Borst

Cover: MMA. 2-5: Wan-go Weng. 6: Hans Hinz, Basel. 10: Wan-go Weng. 12,13: University of California Press. 14,15: Wan-go Weng. 16: BM. 19,20: FGA. 21: Ostasiatiska Museet, Stockholm. 22,23: Seth Joel, N.Y. 24: FGA. 25: (top) Seth Joel, N.Y.; (bottom) Fogg Art Museum, Harvard University. 26,27: FGA. 28-31: Seth Joel, N.Y. 32,33: MMA and Cultural Relics Bureau, Peking. 34-37: Seth Joel, N.Y. 38: Giraudon. 40,41: Bibliothèque Nationale, Paris. 42: MMA and Cultural Relics Bureau, Peking. 43: Francis Lochon/Gamma-Liaison. 44,45: Seth Joel, N.Y. 46: William MacQuitty International Collection, London. 47: Photo Routhier. 48-50: Wan-go Weng. 51,52: William MacQuitty International Collection, London. 53: Cultural Relics Publishing House, Peking. 54,55: MMA and Cultural Relics Bureau, Peking. 56,57: Robert Harding Associates. 58: MMA and Cultural Relics Bureau, Peking. 59: Seth Joel, N.Y. 60-63: Robert Harding Associates. 64: MMA. 66,67: FGA. 68,69: Hans Hinz, Basel. 70: MMA.

71: (left) MMA; (right) Robert Harding Associates. 72: (top) Victoria and Albert Museum, London; (bottom) Wan-go Weng. 73-75: Wan-go Weng. 76,77: William MacQuitty International Collection, London. 78: NPM. 79: Nelson Gallery-Atkins Museum, Kansas City, Mo. 80,81: FGA. 82: Wan-go Weng. 83: MFA. 84,85: Otto Nelson/ Courtesy of Dr. Paul Singer. 86,87: Robert Harding Associates. 88: Louis-Michel Jugie, Paris. 89-91: MMA. 93: Wan-go Weng. 94,95: NPM. 96,97: Wan-go Weng. 98: NPM. 99-101: Percival David Foundation, London. 102: Wan-go Weng. 103: Sotheby Park Bernet and Company, London. 104,105: MFA. 106: NPM. 107: Wan-go Weng. 108: Nelson Gallery-Atkins Museum, Kansas City, Mo. 109: NPM. 110: Wan-go Weng. 111-114: MMA. 115-118: Wan-go Weng. 120: MMA. 121: Wan-go Weng. 122,123: NPM. 124: Paolo Koch/Photo Researchers. 125: BM. 126-128: Wan-go Weng. 129-131: Marc Riboud, Paris. 132-135: Brian Brake/ Photo Researchers. 136: Robert Clarke/Photo Researchers. 137: Joan Lebold Cohen, Cambridge, Mass. 138, 139: EPA/ Scala. 140: MMA. 142: Giraudon. 143: Courtesy of Franco Maria Ricci, Milan. 144,145: Claus Hansmann, Stockdorf. 146,147: Royal Ontario Museum, Toronto. 148: (left) MMA; (right) Marianne Barcelona, N.Y. 149-151: MMA. 152: C.T. Loo Collection, Paris. 153: Wan-go Weng. 154: FGA. 155: Philadelphia Museum of Art. 156,159: NPM. 160,161: Private Collection of the Galerie Regency, Paris. 162,163: Cultural Relics Publishing House, Peking. 164-167: Wan-go Weng. 168,169: Hans Hinz, Basel.

SUGGESTED READINGS

Capon, Edmund and William MacQuitty, *Princes of Jade.* E.P. Dutton and Company, Inc., 1973.

Fairbank, John K. and Edwin O. Reischauer, *China: Tradition and Transformation.* Houghton Mifflin Company, 1978.

Fong, Wen, ed., *The Great Bronze Age in China.* The Metropolitan Museum of Art with Alfred A. Knopf, Inc., 1980.

Gascoigne, Bamber, *The Dynasties and Treasures of China.* Viking Press, Inc., 1973.

Grousset, René, *The Rise and Splendour of the Chinese Empire.* University of California Press, 1952.

Hucker, Charles O., *China's Imperial Past.* Stanford University Press, 1975.

Keswick, Maggie, *The Chinese Garden.* Rizzoli International Publications, Inc., 1966.

Lee, Sherman E., *Chinese Landscape Painting.* Harper and Row Publications, Inc., 1966.

Li, Dun J., *The Ageless Chinese.* Charles Scribner's Sons, 1978.

Smith, Bradley and Wan-go Weng, *China: A History in Art.* Doubleday and Company, 1979.

Sullivan, Michael, *The Arts of China.* University of California Press, 1967.

A NOTE ON USAGE

Since Chinese is not an alphabetic language, any method of rendering Chinese names into English must be approximate. This book uses the traditional and most familiar English spellings: Confucius rather than K'ung-fu-tzu, Peking rather than Pei-ching or the newer Beijing of the *Pin-yin* system now coming into use.

In the Ming and Ch'ing dynasties emperors took reign titles; today these rulers are known by these reign names and not by their personal names. The correct way to refer to Hung-wu, for example, would be as "the Hung-wu emperor." This formality, however, has been dispensed with in *The Emperors of China*.

INDEX

Page numbers in **boldface type** refer to illustrations and captions.

x

Printed and bound in Italy by Arnoldo Mondadori, Verona.

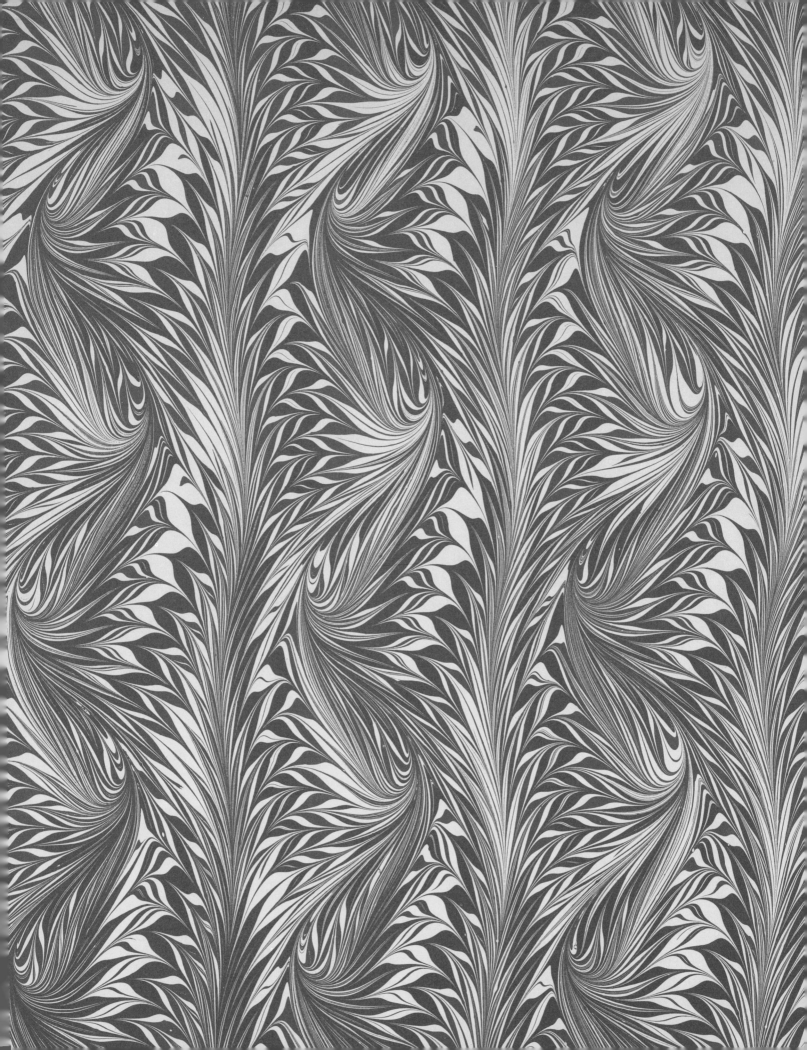